910 West

WORD**PRESS**
quickstart guide

installing, maintaining, and running a successful WordPress blog

ISBN 978-0-557-17758-5

Published by 910 West, LLC.

Printed by Lulu Enterprises, Inc.

TABLE OF
CONTENTS

3

TABLE OF
CONTENTS

WHAT IS WORDPRESS?

WordPress is a web publishing, content management system which was created to make blogging easier. WordPress has been growing in popularity and continues to become more feature rich and easier to use with each new release of the product. The current version of WordPress is 2.8 as of this writing. However, version 2.8 had only been out for a couple of days and therefore this publication will provide examples using WordPress version 2.7.1.

> **NOTE:** *Although the examples will be based on 2.7.1, the features and functions shown will tend to work with the 2.8 version of WordPress. Any major variations in the functionality or processes described will be noted in the text and additional examples for WordPress 2.8 will be placed in Appendix A if necessary.*

WordPress is constantly evolving and new versions are being developed each year. WordPress is built on free, open software which allows programmers and users in the WordPress community to make changes and extend the product to add features and usability.

Because of the very active developer community, WordPress has seen increased use by general website owners. The ability to change and add content without hiring a website developer is creating a new market for WordPress. Not only can you blog and create articles on which people can comment and remark, but users are building their entire websites using WordPress. Because WordPress allows users to edit and create pages very simply, most people are seeing the added benefit of using the WordPress blog publishing platform as a true website creation and content management system.

THE MAKEUP OF A WORDPRESS SITE

There are many modules associated with a WordPress blog. The major parts of a WordPress blog are listed below. These are by no means all there is to a WordPress site, but this is a good starting point for getting to know WordPress.

Posts

A WordPress blog consists of articles you write called posts. Posts are the meat of your WordPress site. The more posts your write, the more content you have and the more interaction you can have with your customers. Posts are displayed in chronological order on your site. Usually the newest post is on top, but that can be changed if desired.

Pages

Your site will also contain pages. These are segregated from the blog where you can relay specific information. Some example pages are the "About Me," "Services," and "Resources" pages. You can have as many pages as your site requires. However, the content on pages does not regularly change and so you should be concentrating on creating "posts" to increase your blog success.

Categories and Tags

WordPress also lets you segregate your posts into Categories and Tags. Categories are very important to the structure and layout of your blog, and should be considered carefully. Categories are broad generalizations of your content while tags are more specific keywords related to your posts. An example for a fitness blog post about working your arms may fall under the "Weight Training" category, and the tags for that same post are more specific like "curls," "biceps," or "arms."

Plugins

WordPress offers a multitude of plugins to extend the functionality of the publishing system. Everything from ensuring you execute proper SEO (Search Engine Optimization) to displaying your latest YouTube video is available. Most plugins are free and are easily installed with just the click of a mouse.

Themes

Themes are like a new skin for your website. When you install a new theme, you are not changing the basic structure of the blog or site, but instead you are adding a different presentation layer onto the existing core functionality. Themes come in many flavors. Two column, three column, and portfolio are but a few. The theme you pick should reflect your style and provide the functionality that best suits your needs.

> **NOTE:** *One of the advantages of using WordPress is the availability of free themes. Although, there are hundreds of free themes to choose from, you may want to consider a Premium theme. Premium themes generally are professionally designed and customizable through an easy point and click interface. Many premium theme houses offer support and free theme upgrades. The cost for a premium theme can range from $25 to $300 depending on the features and designer.*

Comments

Comments are the feedback system of your successful blog. New blogs will struggle to find an audience and may take some time to get people to comment on your posts. Remember that good content allows for good commentary, so writing informative, thought-provoking articles can help you gain a lot of traction and garner multiple comments. Not every post is a masterpiece, so don't be discouraged — keep posting.

This is but an overview of the WordPress system; we will go into more detail in the following chapters. Let's start with getting you prepared to run your WordPress blog.

PREPARING TO
RUN YOUR
WORD**PRESS** BLOG

BEFORE WE CAN RUN WORDPRESS we need to make sure we have a few things in place.

PREREQUISITES

This is the bare minimum needed to install and run your blog. Sure there are many sites that offer you a WordPress blog with your hosting account, but to have full flexibility, we will want to do our own install and customizations. Here is what you need.

A URL

You will need a URL, e.g. *yoursitename.com*. Picking a URL that matches your business name is obviously the best choice. However, sometimes it is not possible, so try your best to pick a URL that best describes your business or the topics of our blog.

A Hosting Account

A hosting account is required to "host" your website. Buying a URL doesn't automatically get you a hosting account, but most likely this is going to be included when you buy your domain. Just about every hosting provider supports running WordPress. If you aren't sure, ask your hosting provider to verify they can run a WordPress blog before you purchase.

A MySQL Database

WordPress needs to store all the information for the blog, such as settings, categories, posts, etc. in a database. WordPress utilizes the free and open database platform called MySQL. If your hosting provider supports WordPress, they will support MySQL. Know your database name.

FTP Access

FTP is short for "file transfer protocol." You will need to ensure that your hosting provider allows you ftp access. To install and manage WordPress this is a must have. Beware of hosting providers that give you a free WordPress blog, but do not offer any ftp access. You are generally limited by the kind of changes you are allowed to make and this can be a problem when you are trying to customize your blog. *Make sure to record your username and password for FTP access to your account. You will need this information to install WordPress.*

If you don't have a hosting plan, we recommend using *www.hostmysite.com*. Their Foundation hosting plan has all of the above and *hostmysite.com* provides excellent 24x7 customer support. *Godaddy.com* also offers plans at discounted rates and since it is the most popular hosting provider, our examples will be based on a *Godaddy.com* account. Each of the above is required to host your own WordPress blog. We're almost ready to install WordPress; all we need now are the tools to transfer files between your computer and the hosting provider's remote computer (*yoursitename.com*).

Download a free FTP program. PC users can use WinSCP *(http://www.winscp.net/eng/download.php)*, which offers a nice GUI interface to your remote server. Mac users can download Cyberduck *(http://cyberduck.ch/)*. Cyberduck has a funny name, but it's a great file management tool.

Now we are ready to begin installation.

INSTALLING WORD**PRESS**

THE INSTALLATION OF WORDPRESS is probably the hardest part about owning and running your own blog. That said, let me reassure you that it is a fairly simple process. Four things must happen:

- You must download the latest version of WordPress.
- A database on your hosting account needs to be created for use with WordPress.
- The WordPress installation files need to be uploaded to your site (Remember, for our example we will use *http://wpbook.info* as our site).
- A 30 second configuration script needs to run on your new site.

Simple steps; let's go through each one.

DOWNLOAD WORDPRESS

Our examples use version 2.7 of WordPress.

> *The newest version is currently 2.8, but the installation process has not changed. Find version 2.7 or 2.8 at* http://wordpress.org/.

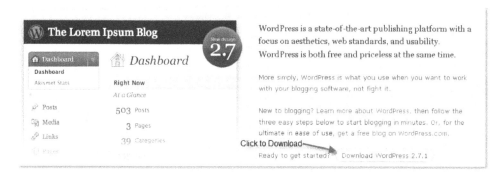

Either Mac or PC version will do. WordPress.org automatically detects which Operating System you are using and provides you with the appropriate download. Our examples will use the PC, but Mac users won't have any problems following along.

Save the file to your hard drive in a location where you can later find it. I suggest creating a folder called "wordpress."

Now we can create a database.

9

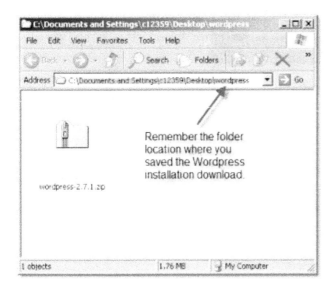

Remember the folder location where you saved the Wordpress installation download.

CREATE A DATABASE

Different hosting providers have different methods to allow you to create a new MySQL database. See your hosting provider's website or online guide to find out what the process is for creating a database. If all else fails, ask them to create one for you.

You'll need to record:

• The database name.
• The database user.
• The database user password.
• The database server name or IP address.

When you create a database, all the information listed above should become apparent and be displayed to you after creation.

Here is an example of the database creation process using one of the most popular hosting provider's (*http:// Godaddy.com*) tools. Of course, your hosting provider will have different screens, but the basic concept is the same.

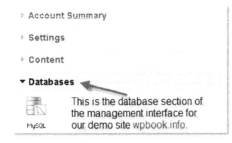

I've already logged in to my account and I am in the management page of my hosting account. I have navigated to the Databases section of the interface.

This is the database section of the management interface for our demo site wpbook.info.

After clicking on the MySQL database icon we are presented with the following screen.

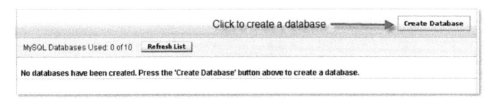

Click on the "Create Database" button.

Give your database a description, choose a username and password. Don't forget to write this information down. WordPress is capable, and runs very well, on Version 5.0 of MySQL. Go ahead and choose version 5. WordPress doesn't need external access, so let's keep it simple and choose "No" on the Direct DB Access. Click "OK" to continue.

Once the Status indicator says "Setup," you're ready to go. Your web host shouldn't take too long to get this setup. They will usually have it ready within an hour or so.

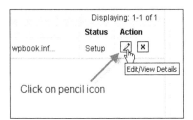

Once you have confirmed the status as "setup," you will need to click on the Edit/View Details icon to record some information.

The info above will be needed in a future step. Please also remember your database password. That information is not displayed on this page.

Step one is complete — give yourself a pat on the back!!!

UPLOAD THE WORDPRESS FILES TO YOUR HOST

By this point, you should have a URL, a hosting plan, and have downloaded both an FTP program and the newest version of WordPress, and have created a database for WordPress.

We are going to begin the file transfer process by unzipping or decompressing the file we downloaded from WordPress.org. Let's go to the location where you saved the file and unzip or decompress them into a new folder.

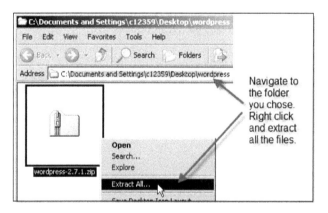

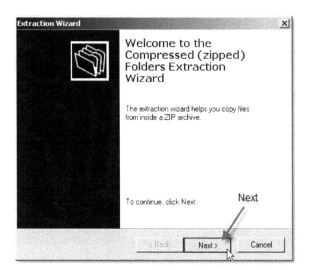

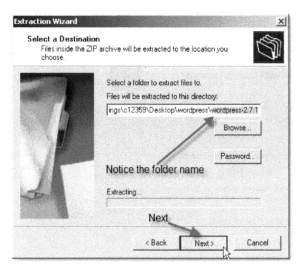

There is no need to change the default folder name, but you may do so if desired. Take note of where it puts the extracted the files.

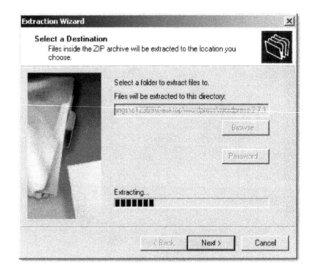

Allow the extraction process to complete.

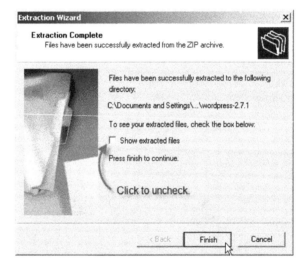

Click "Finish." You can uncheck the box to "Show extracted files." We will be using our FTP program to view and copy the files in the next step.

Now we will need to start the upload. Open your FTP program and enter your host credentials (username and password) to access your site. Our example is using WinSCP, but most FTP programs work about the same.

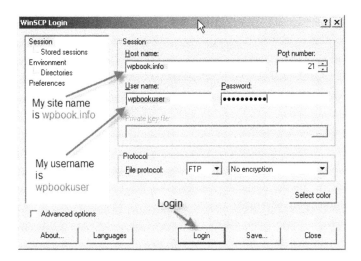

My account details are input into the appropriate fields. Our hostname is the same as our URL which is "wpbook.info." Our username is *wpbookuser* (given to me when I setup my hosting account from *Godaddy.com*). Click "Login" to continue.

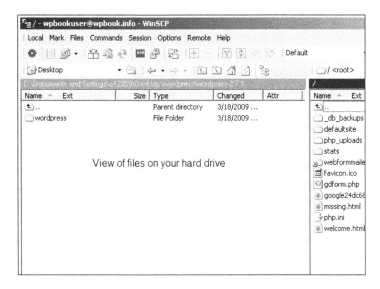

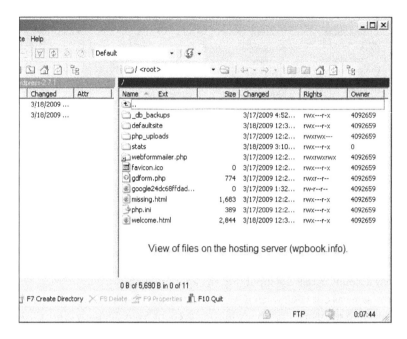

View of files on the hosting server (wpbook.info).

After login in, you should see a list of files on your hard drive, and a list of files that are on your hosting account.

WordPress can be installed in any directory of your choosing. If you will only be running WordPress on your website (which suits 95% of us) then you will need to install the files at the top level directory.

> *This can be confusing at first, but if you don't already have a website setup on your host and this is a new installation, install at the top level. If you have a website already running and are adding a WordPress blog, you can create a directory in which to install WordPress. Like /blog or /interact, etc. If you choose to do this, users who navigate to your blog will use a URL like yoursitename.com/blog or yoursitename.com/interact.*

Godaddy will put a default web page up for you until you are ready to upload your new files and site. We can simply copy our WordPress files over the top of them without harming anything.

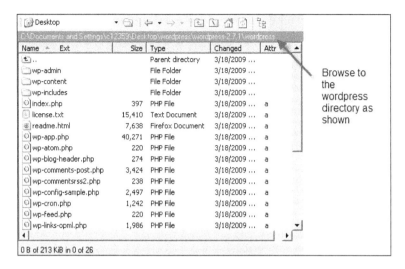

In our FTP client, find the directory where WordPress was extracted and enter the "wordpress" directory.

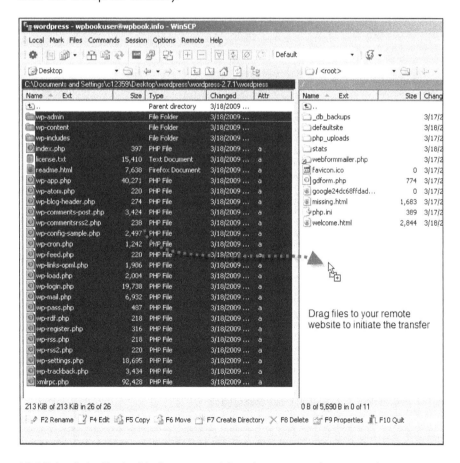

Highlight all the files in this directory and drag them over to the remote site.

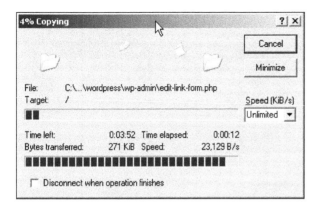

Allow the copy to complete. This could be a long process. Depending on your connection speed this could take anywhere from 1 minute to 10 minutes.

You're done with step 3!

RUN THE CONFIGURATION SCRIPT

Now that the WordPress files have been uploaded to your website we can use our browser to complete the installation.

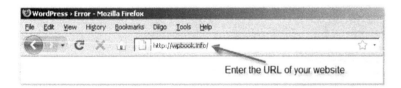

Open your browser and navigate to your site's URL (ours is *wpbook.info*).

Since the site has not been setup before, WordPress will ask you if you want to create a *wp-config.php* file.

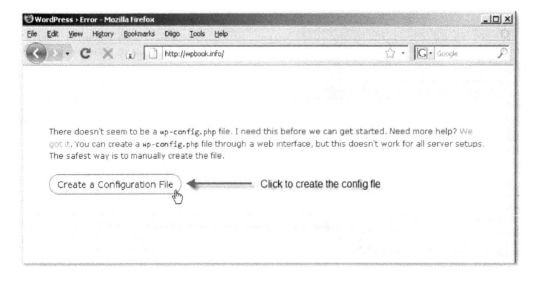

The next screen will ask you to have some info handy. You should have recorded the database info.

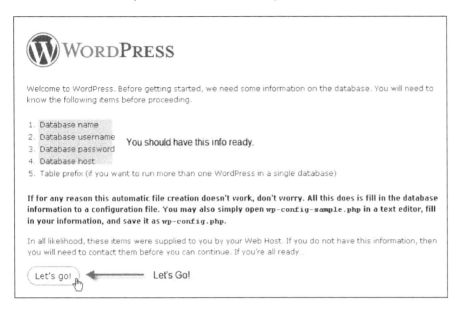

Click "Let's go."

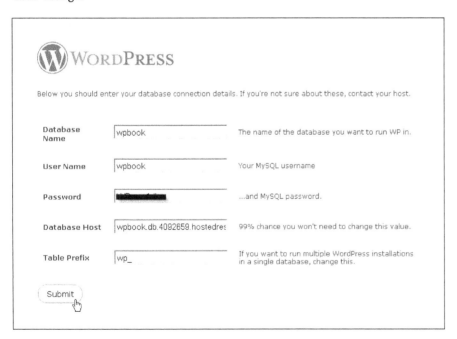

In our particular case, the database name and the user name are identical. Our password has been blocked out for security reasons, and we will use *"wpbook.db.4092659.hostedresource.com"* as the database host. If you have been provided with a different database host, enter that information here. Localhost is the default and in many cases will suffice, but that depends on your hosting provider.

Table Prefix can be anything you like, but the default is fine (change this if more than one WordPress blog is installed on your site). Click "Submit" to continue.

If you get an error after clicking "Submit" then you will have to go back and check your settings and try again. Most often, the username or password is mistyped. If all is good you should see the following screen.

Enter the name of your blog. This can be anything you like. Make sure to enter a valid email address because WordPress will send your username and password. Click "Install WordPress."

You can log in with the above username and password — but we'll go over that in a minute.

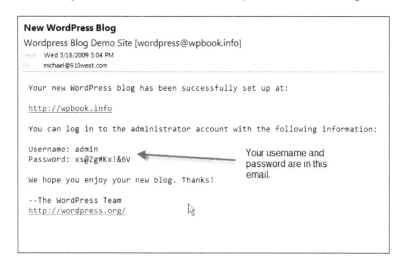

You're done with the installation! How easy was that? Don't forget to check your email for your username and password.

You can change your password later, but you will need to know this one to login for the first time.

QUICK OVERVIEW OF A WORD**PRESS** BLOG

CONGRATULATIONS! You have made it through the hardest part of running your own Word-Press blog. Let's take a look at our handy work and go over a few key areas.

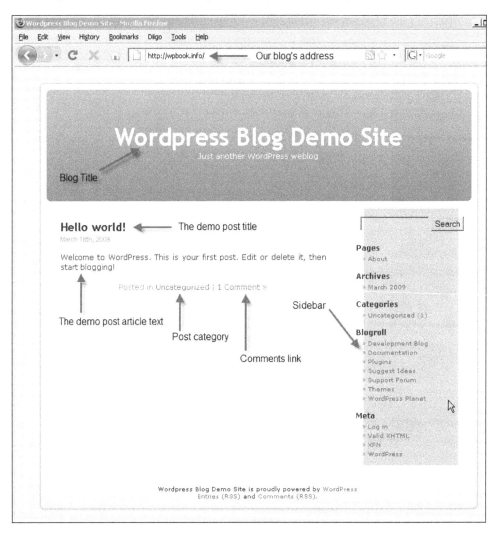

Browse to your blog's address, you will see the default WordPress template.

BLOG TITLE

The blog title is taken from your inputs during the installation process. In our case we wanted to call our blog "Wordpress Blog Demo Site." I'll show you how to change that later if you change your mind.

THE DEMO POST

The latest and only post is "Hello world!" Every WordPress installation comes with this sample post. It is just a short blurb of text for demonstration purposes.

POST CATEGORY

Technically "Uncategorized" is a category according to WordPress. The demo post is "Uncategorized." The number of categories you have will depend on your blog's topic.

SIDEBAR

This template uses a single column sidebar. There are many themes that have 2 and 3 column sidebars. Some themes have sidebars on the right, some on the left, and some on both. You will pick a theme which suites your style the best. We will get into themes later.

COMMENTS LINK

The comments link will direct you to the post's comment section. You, and others who read your blog, can see who has commented on the post and can comment themselves if desired.

The default WordPress install also comes with a demo comment. (See next page.) Each comment has a link for the user who created the comment — this is taken from the submission form's "Website" field. If you do not put a website in this field, your name will not be clickable (cause there is no website you want to associate with your name). The email address is not viewable by anybody but the blog admin. It is used by the administrators to contact users who have made comments (helps deter spam comments, too).

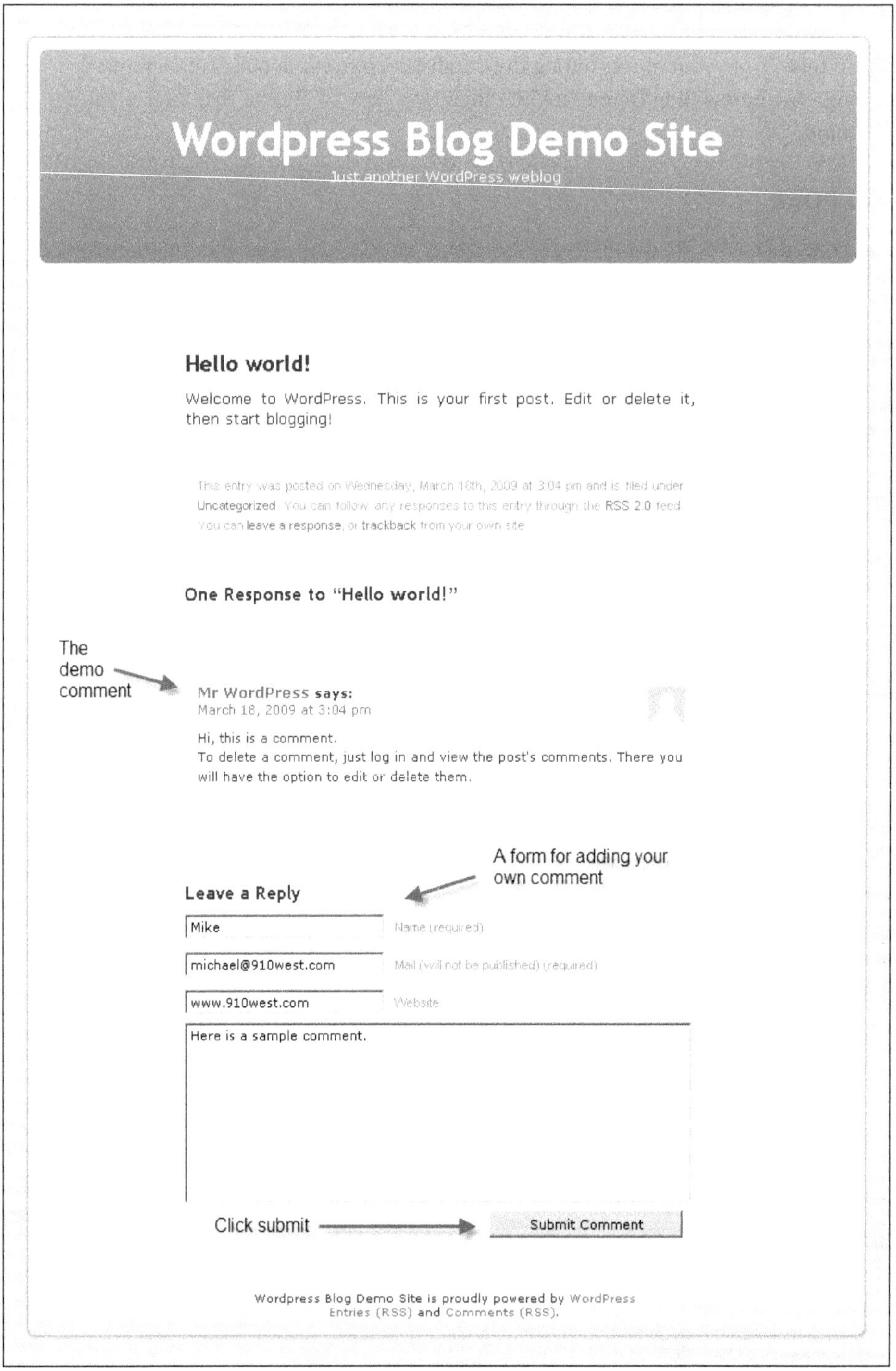

Wordpress Blog Demo Site

Just another WordPress weblog

Hello world!

Welcome to WordPress. This is your first post. Edit or delete it, then start blogging!

This entry was posted on Wednesday, March 18th, 2009 at 3:04 pm and is filed under Uncategorized. You can follow any responses to this entry through the RSS 2.0 feed. You can leave a response, or trackback from your own site.

One Response to "Hello world!"

The demo comment →

Mr WordPress says:
March 18, 2009 at 3:04 pm

Hi, this is a comment.
To delete a comment, just log in and view the post's comments. There you will have the option to edit or delete them.

A form for adding your own comment ←

Leave a Reply

Mike	Name (required)
michael@910west.com	Mail (will not be published) (required)
www.910west.com	Website

Here is a sample comment.

Click submit ——→ Submit Comment

Wordpress Blog Demo Site is proudly powered by WordPress
Entries (RSS) and Comments (RSS).

I've filled out the form with my information. Here is what the post looks like after I commented.

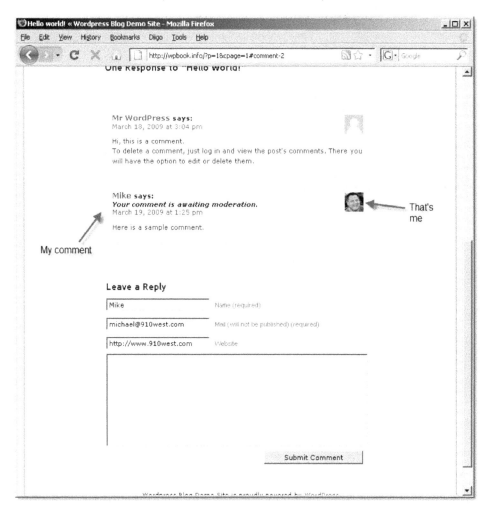

We can see that our comment now appears below the previous comment. By default, all comments are held for moderation. Meaning, once a post receives a comment, you need to take action to allow it to show up in the comments section of the post. This is primarily to avoid spam comments (ads for Viagra, or cellulite cream). We will get into how to moderate comments and change this setting in a later chapter.

Notice my picture next to my comment? I use a service called "Gravatar." The Gravatar service will show profile pictures for those who have signed up with the Gravatar service. The picture is based on the email address used in the comment form. I registered that photo with the email address of Michael@910west.com. This is an optional service and not required and not all blogs are setup to show Gravatars (although the default for WordPress 2.7.x is to enable them).

That's enough on the front end for now. Let's get into the meat of the product by logging in to the management pages for the blog.

QUICK OVERVIEW OF THE WORD**PRESS** MANAGEMENT INTERFACE

IT'S TIME TO MOVE INTO THE MANAGEMENT INTERFACE. To get there we will need to add "/wp-admin" to our blog's URL, e. g. *http://wpbook.info/wp-admin* .

It's a good idea to bookmark this URL so you don't have to try and remember it every time.

Your login page should appear.

We will need to log in with the "admin" username and our initial password.

Once our credentials have been accepted, we are taken to the WordPress dashboard.

THE DASHBOARD

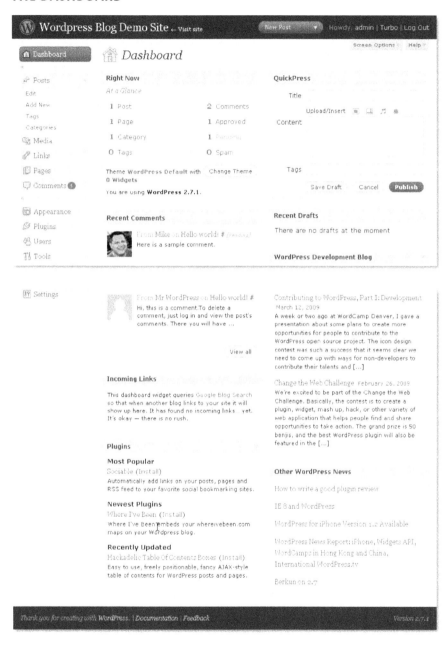

How about an overview of the different parts? We will call these parts "Widgets" in the future. Think of them as little boxes on the admin pages.

Right Now Widget

The Right Now widget shows statistics for your blog. The left side is dedicated to post stats, and the right side is dedicated to comment stats.

QuickPress Widget

The QuickPress widget is a shortcut to writing and publishing a post. Use this when you want to quickly get something on the site.

Recent Comments Widget

As the name implies, it shows the most recent comments made on your blog. Notice that my earlier comment is still pending. I have not approved it and it is still awaiting moderation.

Incoming Links Widget

Incoming Links

This dashboard widget queries Google Blog Search so that when another blog links to your site it will show up here. It has found no incoming links... yet. It's okay — there is no rush.

Other blogs or websites that link back to your posts can sometimes be listed here. Depending on when Google indexes this information, you may not see anything here for a while. The more people that link back to your site, the better for your search engine ranking. I will go into more on Search Engine Optimization later.

Recent Drafts

Recent Drafts

There are no drafts at the moment

Not much to explain here. Just a list of posts you started but did not finish. Look here for a quick way to get back to them.

The Other Widgets

The remaining widgets are put there by WordPress.org developers to bring you news and info about the latest releases of the software.

See Appendix A for version 2.8 changes to the screen options.

🏠 *Dashboard*   Click to show/hide widgets ⟶   Screen Options ⬇   Help ⬇

Show on screen

☑ Right Now   ☑ Recent Comments   ☑ Incoming Links   ☑ Plugins   ☑ QuickPress
☑ Recent Drafts   ☑ WordPress Development Blog   ☑ Other WordPress News

🏠 *Dashboard*   Screen Options ⬇

You can turn them on and off by click on the Screen Options drop-down link at the top of the dashboard and checking/un-checking the appropriate boxes. For now, we'll just leave the defaults.

The Sidebars

There are two sidebars on the left of the Dashboard screen. The top sidebar is sectioned by Posts, Media, Links, Pages, and Comments. The most common areas you will use once the blog is up and running.

The bottom sidebar is for customizing your blog. It contains Appearance, Plugins, Users, Tools and Settings. You won't use many of the options in the bottom sidebar very often after your initial setup.

That's it for the dashboard overview. We'll move on to configuring your blog.

CONFIGURING YOUR WORD**PRESS** BLOG

WE ARE NOW READY to start making configuration changes to the blog.

CHANGE THE ADMIN PROFILE

The randomly generated password is not easy to remember. If you can, more power to you. But for most of us it's a bit cumbersome. Let's change it and give the Admin a bit more personality.

To access the profile panel find the bottom sidebar and expand the "Users" dropdown.

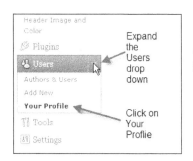

Expand the Users drop down

Click on Your Profile

After expanding the "Users" dropdown click on "Your Profile." The Profile page appears.

I'm assuming you are logged in as Admin. If you would like to change the password for other users, click on "Authors and Users."

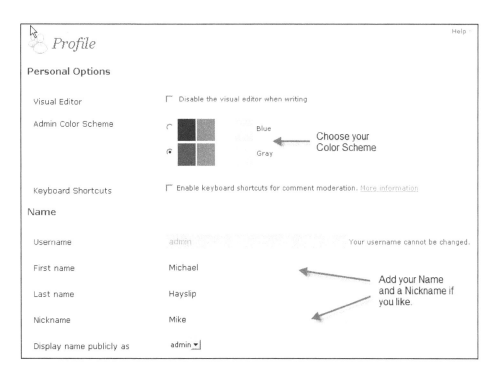

The top half of the profile page allows you to change the color scheme of the management interface. Add your name and choose a nickname (usually just your first name) or leave it blank.

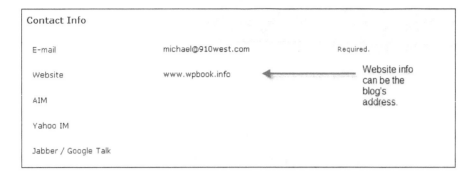

The Contact portion allows you to change your email address if needed. The address you entered during the install process is listed by default. Also, you should enter a website address. This can be and usually is the blog's address.

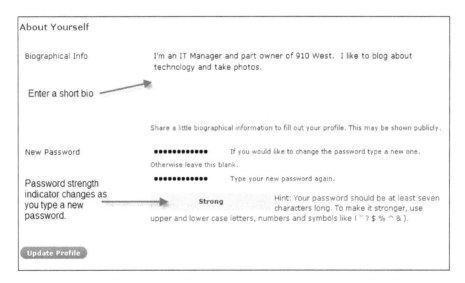

Finish the process by entering a short bio and changing your password. The default password that was generated during the install is a "Strong" password. You should try to choose a password that is in the medium to strong range.

Click on "Update Profile" and wait for the profile update message to appear before continuing.

Now that you have saved your changes, it is time to decide how you want your name to appear on the site. If you go back to the name section of the profile page, you now have the option to choose from the Display Name Dropdown. The public display name is what is shown to users on the site. For example, if you author a post, this name will be used for the "Written by:" information. Showing readers a "Written by: admin" post is a little impersonal and should reflect the author's name or nickname.

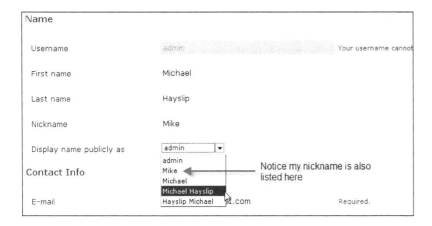

Notice that my nickname is also listed here. Pick the name you want displayed publicly and click on "Update Profile" to save.

GENERAL SETTINGS

Now that your profile is complete, we can move on to the General settings.

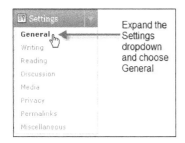

Expand the Settings dropdown located on the bottom sidebar and click on "General." The General Settings page is displayed.

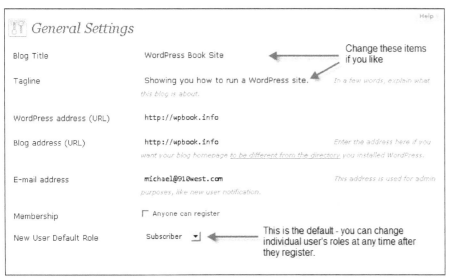

You can modify the information if you like. I have decided to change the Blog Title and the Tagline for *wpbook.info*.

Notice the New User Default Role dropdown. This is the default role that is assigned to users when they register (if you allow registrations). It is also the default role assigned when an administrator adds users via the "Authors and Users" settings. For now, leave it at the default. We can always change a user's role anytime after an account has been created.

For those who are curious about what the different roles are, here is a brief explanation.

- *Administrators can change anything on the blog. This includes removing users and changing the blog title or theme. They have no restrictions.*
- *Editors can do anything related to the blog's publishing. That includes adding and deleting posts, managing categories, editing posts, and approving and deleting comments.*
- *Authors can write, publish and delete posts and comments on posts they create.*
- *Contributors can write posts, but cannot publish them (an editor or above must publish for them). They can only delete posts they have written and approve or delete comments on posts they have written.*
- *Subscribers can only read. Not very useful as a user, but can be good if you want input on posts you have not published. They can read and get back to you with feedback.*

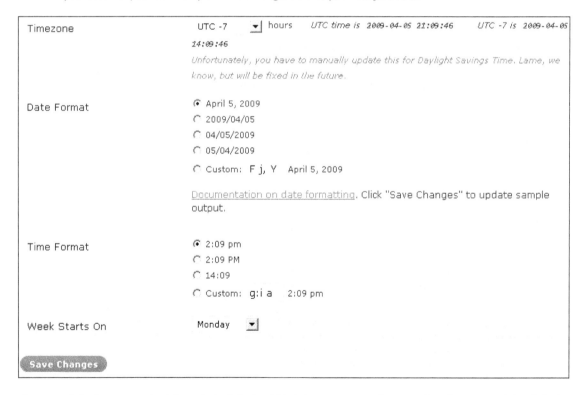

The rest of the inputs can be left at their defaults. This is just a matter of personal preference and the defaults usually are good enough.

Make sure to "Save Changes" if you modify anything.

WRITING SETTINGS

Next is the Writing Settings. Click on "Writing" in the Settings sidebar widget.

The Writing Settings are displayed below.

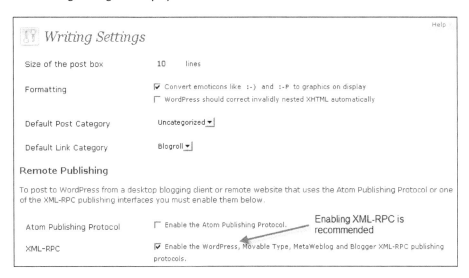

Changing the post box size will give you a little more room when writing posts. Ten lines are usually fine, but you can modify this later if you prefer.

The formatting checkboxes are a matter of preference. Most choose to leave these at their default values.

Remote Publishing

WordPress allows you to publish posts from external tools. There are third party desktop applications that allow you to write, edit, create and modify posts without logging into your WordPress management site. If at a later date you decide to use some remote publishing tools, you will need to enable these settings. For now, let's enable XML-RPC, the most common method of remote publishing.

Post via E-mail

Post via e-mail allows you to send (you guessed it) emails to the address you specify above and have the contents of the message appear on your blog as a new post. The Subject line is used as the post title while the body is used as the post content.

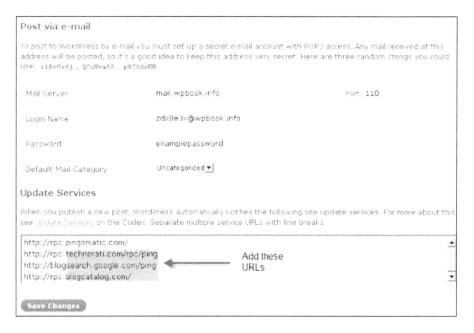

Check with your hosting provider for info on your mail server, but it is usually some combination of *"mail.<yourdomainname>"* or perhaps *mailhost.<yourdomain>*. You will need to create an email account that matches the one you entered in the above Login Name field. If you don't intend to use this feature, you can leave the default values in place.

Update Service

You should also add additional information in the Update Services text box. By default, your blog will notify *rpc.pingomatic.com* about new posts. The following should also be added:

http://rpc.technorati.com/rpc/ping
http://blogsearch.google.com/ping
http://rpc.blogcatalog.com/

Adding these additional ping services will improve the likelihood that your posts will show up in blog searches. The more services you notify, the more chances that people will find your blog.

Make sure to click on "Save Changes" when you have completed your modifications.

READING SETTINGS

You will find the Reading Settings in the Settings sidebar widget. Click on "Reading."

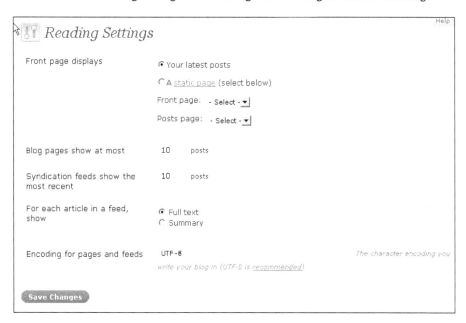

We won't change anything here for now. The most powerful feature here is the Front page displays setting. You can choose to have the front page show your latest blog posts or a static page.

> *Remember in our introduction we discussed how WordPress is a powerful content management system and can not only be used for blogs, but also a full featured website? Here is an example of where changing the front page to a static page may make sense. For instance, you may want the first page a reader visits to be your business's "About" page instead of the blog.*

Let's leave the settings as is for now.

DISCUSSION SETTINGS

The Discussion Settings are probably most useful to us right now. Discussion is another word for Comments in WordPress lingo. We definitely want to take a look at how we handle comments on our blog. Find and click on the Discussion link in the Settings sidebar widget.

```
                                                                              Help
  ┌─┐
  │⁑│ Discussion Settings
  └─┘

  Default article settings       ☑ Attempt to notify any blogs linked to from the article (slows down posting.)
                                  ☑ Allow link notifications from other blogs (pingbacks and trackbacks.)
                                  ☑ Allow people to post comments on the article
                                  (These settings may be overridden for individual articles.)

  Other comment settings          ☑ Comment author must fill out name and e-mail
                                  ☐ Users must be registered and logged in to comment

                                  ☐ Automatically close comments on articles older than  14       days

                                  ☐ Enable threaded (nested) comments  5 ▾ levels deep

                                  ☑ Break comments into pages with  50      comments per page and the  last ▾
                                  page displayed by default
                                  Comments should be displayed with the  older ▾  comments at the top of each page

  E-mail me whenever              ☑ Anyone posts a comment
                                  ☑ A comment is held for moderation
```

Allowing your blog to notify others when you have linked to one of their posts is generally a good practice and shows that you are considerate of other blogs when linking to them.

When others link to your blog while pingbacks and trackbacks are enabled you will be notified via the comments functionality of the blog. Each blog that links back to your post will show up as a comment.

Of course, you can disable comments by default, but you probably want the interaction with your audience.

The Other comment settings should be looked at closely. At a minimum we want to have comment authors to fill out name and email. This helps with spam and encourages folks to be accountable for what they say.

Having folks register before they can comment will slow down the commenting process and may discourage users from posting comments.

You can choose to enable threaded comments which will allow others to comment on a comment. Say Joe has commented on your post and has asked a question, Jill can choose to reply to Joe's comment rather than comment on your post. Some bloggers like this feature, others find it too cumbersome — your choice.

You should elect to get an email when folks comment. If you don't, you will have to log into your blog's administration pages to find out if someone has commented or if a comment is awaiting moderation. Readers want to know that someone is actively watching the blog, and if you wait too long before you approve comments, readers will think the blog is stale.

Spam Prevention

The following settings have been introduced to deter spam. By now you have heard me mention spam about a thousand times and may be wondering how spam can get on your blog. Here is a brief explanation:

> *It has become apparent that the more sites that link back to your site, the more popular and the higher ranking your website will become in search engines. Spammers have figured this out as well and are using automated programs to search the Internet, find blogs, and submit comments (we refer to these as spam bots). They usually have links back to their website(s) embedded in their comment. These programs comment on thousands and thousands of blogs and are generally considered a nuisance. They use fake names and fake email addresses and their comments usually do not add any value to the conversation and are generic enough to apply to any and all articles. E.g. "You have a great blog. Keep up the good work" or "Can you tell me where I can find more information on this?" As a blog owner, you are tasked with ensuring that spam is eliminated from your blog. If you ignore the spam, your readers will become annoyed and stop visiting and it gives the impression that you're asleep at the wheel.*

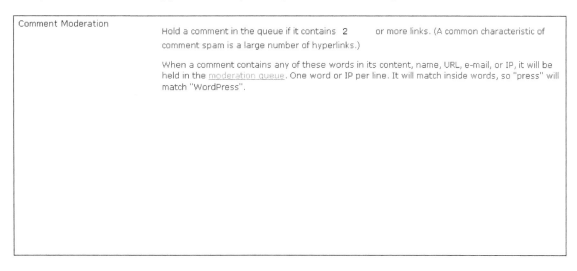

Electing to have an administrator approve every comment can be a little overwhelming for a one- or two-person blog. If you have a large blog with multiple authors and administrators, this choice may be viable.

Requiring comment authors to have a previously approved comment is a nice compromise. This prevents spam from appearing on your blog, and also allows those "regular" comment authors to post freely. We assume that if they have had a comment approved in the past, they are not considered spammers.

Comment Moderation settings can be left at the default. Most legitimate comment authors will not have a need to post more than two links to any comment. Maybe you are asking your readers to provide you with the URLs of some of their favorite websites; in this case they may post more than two which will hold the comment in the moderation queue. You can always approve the comment later if it seems legitimate.

You can leave the large textbox blank for now. Spammers are very clever and won't use the common spellings of words anymore. They will use words like "Vgra" or "Viaggrra;" words that are close enough so you know what they are hocking, but too much trouble to try and put into a list. If your blog is getting the same spam over and over again, then this can be useful, but you should wait to see what kind of spam you are attracting before you make any decisions about what you should list here.

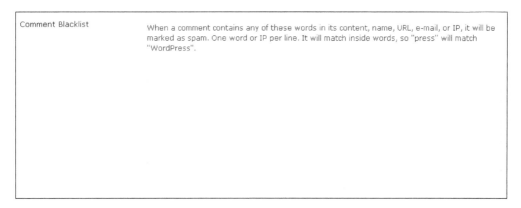

The same goes for the Comment Blacklist. Adding items here will mark them as spam right away and won't place them in the comment moderation queue.

Avatars

Avatars are the little icons that show up next to the comments that people author. If you elect to turn them on, you should also make sure that your avatar is pleasing and friendly. You will also be commenting on your own blog (as replies to other comments). You will want to sign up for the free Gravatar service which was created by the same people who created WordPress. Visit their website at *http://gravatar.com* to sign up.

Gravatars work by looking up the email address you supply when commenting and associating that email address with your "avatar." You can have multiple email addresses and associate different photos with them. Here is what my Gravatar account looks like.

I have added two email addresses and associated the same photo for each. Sometimes I comment as *mike@itdoescompute.com* and other times as *michael@910west.com*. In either case, readers can see what I look like and it adds a personal touch.

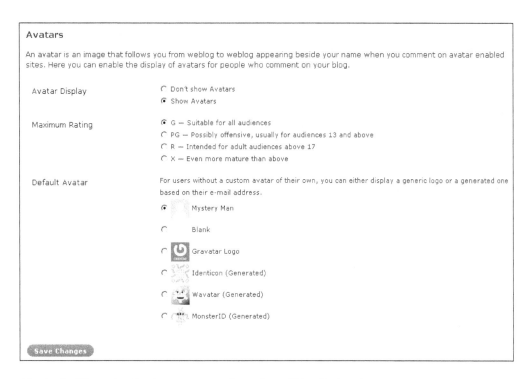

Also in the Discussion Settings, you can select what will be displayed as an avatar.

Make sure to "Save Changes" after you have made your modifications.

MEDIA SETTINGS

Find the Media Settings under in the Settings sidebar. Click to display the Media Settings page.

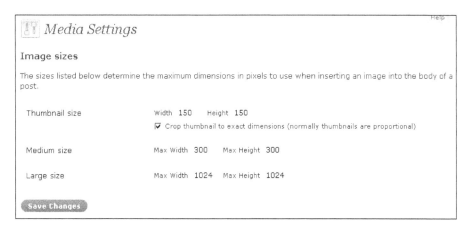

Media Settings apply to images that you upload and use in your blog posts. Thumbnails are smaller versions of images that give you an idea of what the associated larger photo looks like. It is a teaser to encourage readers to click to view the full size image. The medium and large size settings can be left at their defaults. You can always come back later and change these settings if necessary. Most find that the defaults are generally fine.

PRIVACY SETTINGS

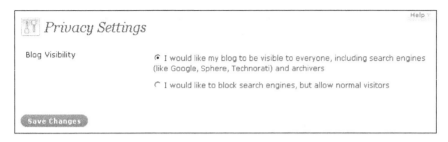

There is nothing special about these options. This option was set during the installation process. You can change it here if you like.

PERMALINK SETTINGS

Permalinks are pretty important to a blog's search engine friendliness. A permalink is the permanent link to a post or page. E.g. *http://wpbook.info/2009/04/how-to-install-wordpress* is a much friendlier URL than *http://wpbook.info/?p=123*. Search engines also like friendly names, too.

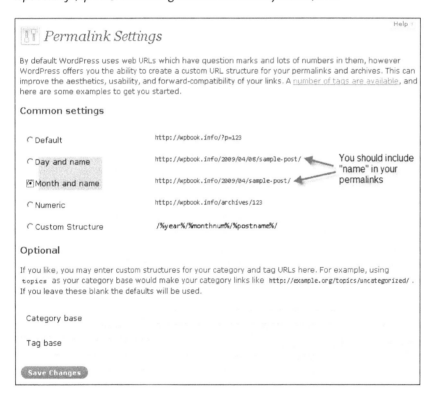

You should try to make the URL for your posts reflect the post's topic. Having the "name" included in your permalinks is recommended. When people see a link they want to have some idea about what they will find after clicking through. A friendly permalink name will give them a hint.

Choose either the "Day and name" or "Month and name" option. I have selected the "Month and name" option here.

Changing category and tag base is not necessary. This defaults to *http://wpbook.info/category/* and *http://wbook.info/tag/*. We'll talk a bit more about categories and tags later. You can change these default values at any time.

MISCELLANEOUS SETTINGS

It is not recommended to change the Miscellaneous Settings. The current defaults will suffice.

Uploads of photos and videos you may need for your posts are stored in the wp-content/uploads folder. If you do not change this setting, the URL path to files does not need to be modified either.

You should organize your uploads by month and year to keep things nice and neat. You probably don't want all uploaded files to appear under one folder as the many files can be cumbersome to sort or find.

> **NOTE:** *You most likely won't need to browse your web server's uploads directory since this functionality is handled by the WordPress posting interface. More advanced web developers and programmers that you may hire to do customization will appreciate the organization.*

That's it. You have gone through each of the settings options for a default WordPress installation. We may come back to some of these settings as we progress in our blogging, but you can take a break and relax for a few before we move on to Plugins.

PLUGINS

WordPress plugins were created to add functionality to WordPress. Plugins are an extension of the core functionality and can be updated, de-activated, or uninstalled at will. There are a few plugins that are recommended. I'll show you how to find and install a few plugins as we continue through the chapter. Find the Plugins management area on the bottom sidebar and expand the dropdown.

Click on "Installed" to view your blog's currently installed plugins. The default WordPress 2.x installation comes with the Akismet and "Hello Dolly" plugins.

See Appendix A for version 2.8 changes to the Manage Plugins Screen.

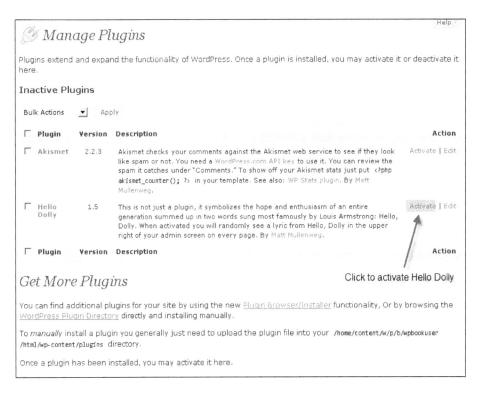

The version, description, and actions you can perform on each plugin are displayed. We will start with the Hello Dolly plugin.

Hello Dolly

Click on the "Activate" link for Hello Dolly and notice how the management page changes.

Take a look at the top right of your administrator screen and notice some new text. After activating the plugin, you now have new functionality. The functionality that Hello Dolly adds is minimal, but fun. Notice now that the Hello Dolly plugin is listed under Currently Active Plugins, while Akismet is still in the Inactive Plugins section of this management page. Now that Hello Dolly is active, you can deactivate it if you wish.

Akismet

The Akismet plugin adds super spam catching capabilities and is definitely a must have if you are going to allow comments on your blog. Akismet keeps a collection of known spammer identities and website addresses on their servers. The plugin collects this information and evaluates comments made on your site and determines whether they are spam and marks them accordingly. If it makes a mistake, you can set a comment as "not spam" and have it learn and try to correct its mistakes in the future. Also, if it doesn't find something that is clearly spam, you can mark it as spam and allow Akismet to add that pattern to its database to better protect you and everyone else who uses Akisment to deter spam. Activate Akismet now.

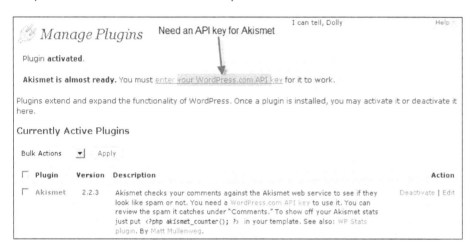

Notice now that Akismet is listed under Currently Active Plugins; however, it is not ready to start catching spam yet. We need to get our API key from *WordPress.com*. It only takes a minute or two to get an API key. Head over to *http://en.wordpress.com/api-keys.*

Sign up for a new account. If you already have an account on *WordPress.com*, you can skip this part and login to *WordPress.com* with your current username and password.

Choose a username and password you can remember. In this case I have chosen the name of the blog for the username. You may use the API key on more than one blog (as long as the blog is owned by you). In that case you will want a username that is more generic than the blog name. Click "Next" to proceed.

Check Your Email to Complete Registration

An email has been sent to michael@wpbook.info to activate your account. Check your inbox and click the link in the message. It should arrive within 30 minutes. If you do not activate your account within two days, you will have to sign up again.

You will need to check your email account to confirm your registration.

Click the link in the email to activate the account.

Your new account username and password is displayed. Click the login link to grab our new API key.

NOTE: *WordPress.com is a free service in which you can start a free blog. The interface will seem very similar to your own blog's, however WordPress.com does not offer you the customizability that hosting your own WordPress blog offers. Just remember which site you are logged on to and try not to get confused. You will only need to logon to WordPress.com to get the API key for Akismet. You do of course have the option to blog on WordPress.com as well l as your own. You could start blogging about a completely different topic if you wish.*

Click login to see the Dashboard.

Click on the Profile link in the sidebar to see view your API key.

Your API key is displayed at the top of the page. Make sure to copy the key before proceeding.

On our own blog, we will need to go back to Plugins to enter our API key.

Click the link to apply the key.

Paste the API key in the text box and click on "Update options."

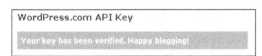

If you entered the key correctly, you should get a nice message saying that the key has been verified.

That's it for Akismet. The plugin is ready to catch spam.

Now let's move on to finding and installing new plugins.

ADDITIONAL PLUGINS

There are a few additional plugins that are recommended for a new Word-Press blog.

They are:

- ***All in One SEO Pack*** – for increasing Search Engine Optimization.
- ***Google XML Sitemaps*** – to allow Google and other search engines to index your site's content more easily.
- ***FD Feedburner Plugin*** – to help you track your RSS subscribers. More discussion on RSS and tracking your readers will come later.
- ***WordPress Database Backup*** – allows you to backup your WordPress data in case of a problem or just for peace of mind. This is useful for getting a backup just before doing a WordPress upgrade.

These are but a few additional plugins that are a must have. We'll go through the installation of these plugins, but if you want more functionality, or find a plugin you can't live without, you'll have the experience needed to install more plugins on your blog.

Installing plugins has been streamlined in this version of WordPress. There are two methods used to install plugins — the search method and the .zip method. We will concentrate on using the search method because it saves us a step in that we don't have to go collecting a bunch of zip files. The search method will find the plugins for us and help us.

You will need to find the Plugins section of the sidebar.

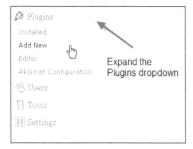

Expand the dropdown and click on "Add New" to begin an installation. We will find and install all the plugins we will need before going back to activate and configure them. This will keep us focused and keep us from jumping around from interface to interface.

All in One SEO Pack

In the search box enter "all in one seo" and click search.

You should see your search results displayed in the browser.

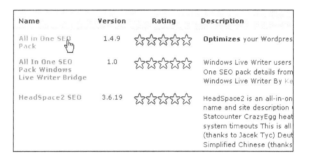

We want to click on the "All in One SEO Pack" link that is our first hit.

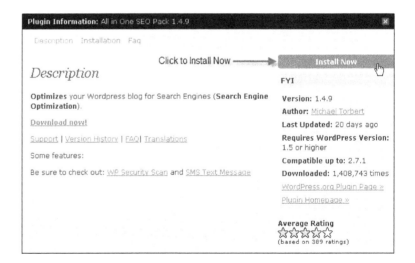

A pop-up window appears and gives you some details about the plugin you are about to install. You can read the description, installation, or faq tabs. Click "Install Now" to install the plugin.

After a few moments you should see a success page for the All in One SEO Pack. Remember, we are going to install all the plugins first before activating, so click on the "Return to Plugins page" link to proceed to install the next plugin.

Google XML Sitemaps

Remember to click on the "Add New" link to continue. Enter "Google XML Sitemaps" in the search box and click "Search."

Find Google XML Sitemaps in the search results and click the link to install.

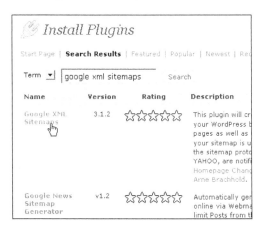

> *Don't worry about the Warning message that is displayed. I have been running this plugin on multiple 2.7.1 WordPress blogs without incident. In fact, I believe the author has ensured compatibility with 2.7 which is only one minor version below 2.7.1*

Click the "Install Now" link.

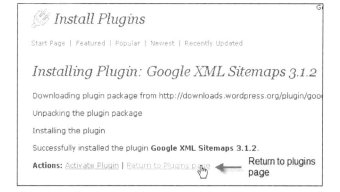

When the installation is complete, please return to the Plugins page.

FD Feedburner Plugin

Okay, by now you should be familiar with installing plugins. I won't show you screen shots for the two that are left, but I'll tell you what to do.

- Make sure to click on the "Add New" link to continue.
- Enter "FD Feedburner" into the search box and click "Search."
- Click on the "FD Feedburner" link in the search results window.
- Click "Install Now" to complete the installation.

Return to the Plugins page.

WordPress Database Backup

Now let's install the final plugin.

Click the "Add New" link.

Enter "WordPress Database Backup" in the search box and click "Search."

Find and click on the "WP-DB-Backup" link in the search results.

Click "Install Now" to complete the installation.

Return to the Plugins page so we can start activating our newly installed plugins.

ACTIVATING YOUR NEWLY INSTALLED PLUGINS

Now that you are back at the plugins page, you can see the list of currently active plugins in green while the normally colored inactive plugins are listed below them.

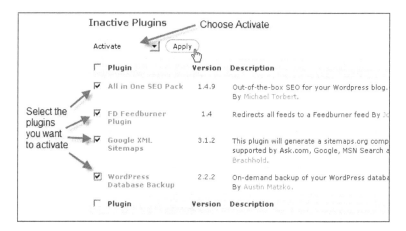

We need to do a Bulk Action of Activate — please choose Activate from the drop-down menu. Select all the plugins you want to activate at this time. For now, we want to activate all 4 of the plugins we just installed and click "Apply."

After a few seconds you will see the above message indicating that your plugins are activated — congratulations.

CHANGING PLUGIN SETTINGS/OPTIONS

Most plugins have an administration page where you can set options or change settings and configurations.

All in One SEO

Let's start by making some changes to the All in One SEO plugin's options. You will find the options page for the All in One SEO plugin in the Settings dropdown on the bottom sidebar.

Expand the Settings dropdown menu and find and click on the "All in One SEO" link. The All in One SEO plugin has a lot of customizable options. Don't worry — the default values for most of these are just fine for our purposes and the built-in help links give us some good information about what each option means.

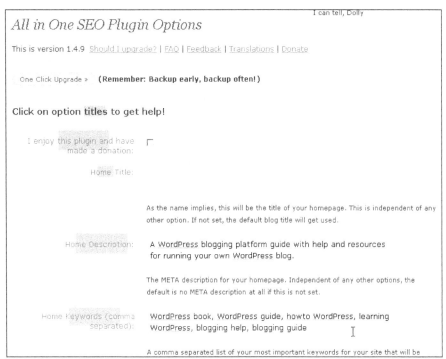

Notice that you can click on the titles to get some explanations for each option.

Donation

The makers of this plugin offer it for free. If you wish to make a small donation, click the "Donate" link above and be sure to check the box.

Home Title

Change the Home Title if you want your WordPress site's homepage to have a different title than your blog. Probably not, but the option is available if you decide you need it.

Home Description

Add a brief description of what your WordPress blog site is about. Your description should be brief, but also give a fair description of your blog.

Home Keywords

Choose 8 to 10 keywords or phrases that describe your blog's topics. These keywords may be indexed by some search engines and therefore will be associated with your blog when users perform a search.

The rest of the All in One SEO options work well right out of the box, but you should definitely take a quick look at each option and read the brief descriptions by clicking on each of the tiles.

Google XML Sitemaps

The Google XML Sitemaps plugin is used to generate a sitemap file so that search engines can easily identify and index your site. The plugin also generates the sitemap after your blog changes depending on the frequency that has been chosen. The plugin's options can be found in the Settings section of the bottom sidebar.

There are a bunch of options to choose here as well, but we don't need to change any right now. You can review the options on your own but we need to generate our sitemap now.

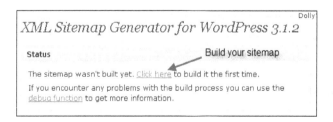

Find the status box at the top of the page and click to build your sitemap for the first time.

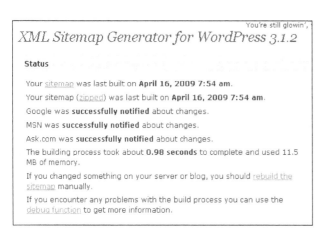

After clicking the link you should see a screen similar to the one above. We can leave this plugin alone from now on unless we decide to make major changes like adding pages, changing the directory where the blog is installed, making the homepage a static page, etc.

WordPress Database Backup

The WordPress Database Backup plugin will help you make a backup of your current WordPress site. Remember, all of your content is stored in a data-base. If you need to move hosting providers, or you have somehow deleted all of your posts, you can recover using the backups created by this plugin.

To setup the WordPress Database Backup plugin, you must navigate and expand the Tools dropdown in the sidebar.

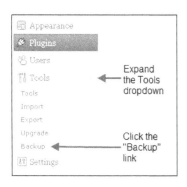

Click the "Backup" link to bring up the Options page for the plugin.

Tables

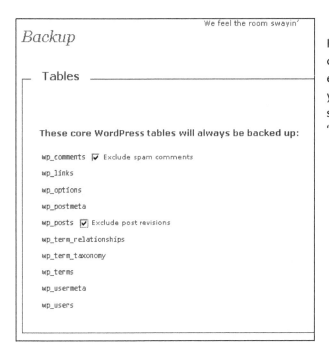

In the Tables section, you have the option to exclude the spam comments (who wants to recover those), and the post revisions. Every change you make to a post is recorded in the database, so if you value that information, make sure to "uncheck" the box.

Backup Options

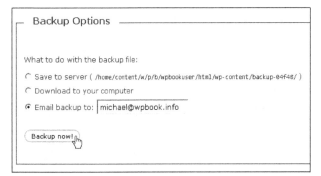

These options are for an immediate backup. Let's do a backup now by selecting the email option and clicking "Backup now!"

After a few seconds you should see a progress bar start to appear.

Wait until the progress bar reaches 100% before proceeding.

Scheduled Backups

It is a good idea to configure a scheduled backup. Weekly is often sufficient. If you write a large number of posts each day, you may want to set a higher frequency.

Click the "Schedule backup" link to continue.

Check your email. You should receive email from your WordPress site on a regular basis with the backup as an attachment. Save the email for as long as you think you may need that backup.

FD Feedburner Plugin

I have saved the most complicated plugin configuration for last. The plugin requires that you understand what RSS is and why it may be important to you. Once you understand RSS you will understand what the FD Feedburner Plugin is doing.

RSS Overview

What is RSS? The letters RSS stand for Really Simple Syndication. Syndication of your content (in this case your blog posts) is the goal of RSS, and syndication means that your content is seen by more people. An RSS feed (which is a term you will hear a lot) allows publishers to make updates to their content available to anyone that subscribes. The word subscribe sounds like there will be money exchanged, but that is not the case. Subscribing to an RSS feed is free and easy.

If a site offers an RSS feed, you will most often see a symbol that resembles the following.

Clicking on an icon similar to the one above will allow you to subscribe to the website's feed. Once subscribed, you will receive content that is published by this website automatically in your RSS reader.

> *One thing to note is that RSS feeds can be offered via email and a lot of people prefer to get new content via email. I'll give you some instructions for allowing your blog to be read via email a little later in this section.*

RSS readers are available for free and can be used on the web or via a desktop application. Try *http://google. com/reader* or *http://bloglines.com* for some nice online versions. Many people elect to use online readers vs. desktop readers because they allow you to access your feeds from more than one computer and keep them synchronized online.

If you subscribe to an RSS feed for a particular website, you do not need to visit that website each day to see if there is new content. Your RSS reader will detect changes to the feed and present them to you in a single interface where you can categorize and sort according to your needs. This is why RSS is very popular and often the way most people consume website content.

Can you offer an RSS feed of your content? Sure. The most important thing to note is that your WordPress blog already has feeds built in to the publishing system. WordPress blogs offer RSS feeds for all articles, just a single category, or only comments.

Since RSS has become so popular, the issue has become how to track how many people are subscribed to your feeds. That's why we have Feedburner.

Feedburner is a free service now offered by Google that can track your subscriber count. It is easy to setup and can provide valuable information about your readers.

When you sign up for a Feedburner account, you will need to provide the URL for your blog's feed to start tracking subscribers. Once you provide that URL to Feedburner, you will need to direct all your feed traffic to Feedburner to collect stats. This is why the FD Feedburner Plugin in so handy.

The FD Feedburner Plugin will convert any clicks on your site's feed URL to the newly created Feedburner URL. There is no coding involved on your part because the plugin does all the work for you.

Feedburner Setup

You must first tell Feedburner the URL of your blog's feed. In your browser, go to *http://feedburner.google.com* and enter your Google ID and password to login. If you do not already have one, simply sign up for a new account.

> **NOTE:** *You will need your Google Account login information again later. Please record your account username and password.*

Once you are logged in, you will see a box in which to enter your feed's URL. You will most likely find your blog's RSS feed at *http://<yourblogsurl>/?feed=rss2*. Mine is *http://wpbook.info/?feed=rss2*. Notice that the */?feed=rss2* portion is the same. Our WordPress 2.7.1 installation supports version 2 of the RSS protocol and therefore we will use that. If you have any doubts about this or using the above syntax doesn't seem to work when you click "Next," simply enter your blog's URL without the /?*feed=rss2* and let Feedburner try to detect your feed's URL.

Now that you have entered a valid feed URL, you will be asked to confirm the information for Feed Title, and Feed Address. Feed Addresses cannot contain any spaces. A good address is short and provides a little guidance about what to find in your RSS feed.

That's it! You now have a feed that can be tracked by Feedburner. Click "Next" to continue.

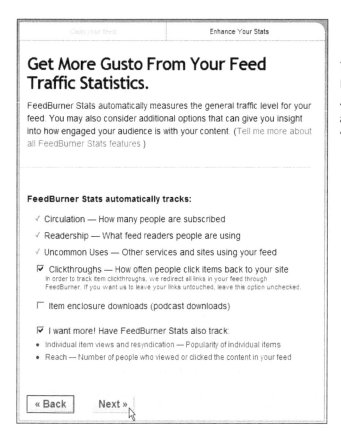

You'll want to track clickthroughs and have Feedburner track individual items and reach. At this stage we are not podcasters, but can always come back and track those later. Click "Next" to continue.

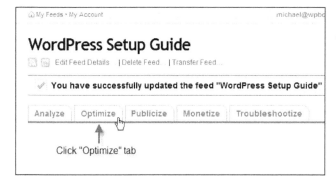

Just a couple more steps. Click the "Optimize" tab to make our feed compatible and reader friendly.

Optimize Your Feed

Sometimes your feed just wants to look good. Spruce it up in the following ways:

Give Your Feed Legs

* Reach the widest possible audience by consolidating your subscription links into one feed that works in any reader, on the desktop, web, mobile devices and beyond. SmartFeed™ goes with everything.

           ← Activate

Podcast Feeds Are Pretty Feeds

* SmartCast™ enables feeds from any blogging tool or platform for podcasting.

Feed Accessories Are All The Rage

* Let's face it — a raw XML file isn't the best looking guy/gal in the room. Offer your audience handy instructions and one-click subscription options with BrowserFriendly. ←———— Activate

* Splice in your Flickr or Buzznet photos for picture-perfect posts.

* Share your collected del.icio.us, Furl or Bloglines links.

* Publicize your location using fashionable latitude and longitude Geotags.

At a minimum, we will need to activate the SmartFeed option and the BrowserFriendly option.

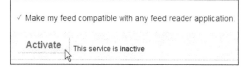

Click to "Activate" SmartFeed.

BrowserFriendly

Make it easy for potential subscribers to preview and subscribe to your text or podcast feed. Applies clean visual formatting to the eyesore of raw feed XML for much improved readability in all modern web browsers.

Take the default settings for BrowserFriendly except for the Personal Message option. Change this if you desire. Click "Save" to continue.

Remember when I mentioned that it was possible for readers to get RSS feeds via email? Well, you can setup the feature to allow your readers this option by enabling this feature in Feedburner.

Clicking the "Publicize" tab and find the "Email Sub-scriptions" link on the right.

Activate the Email Subscriptions by clicking the "Activate" button. Once you activate, you will need to complete the setup for each of the items on the sidebar on the left side of the "Publicize" page.

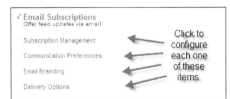

Subscription Management – most people don't need to change the settings here. You probably do want to check the box to receive an email when somebody subscribes via email.

Communication Preferences – since email subscriptions are a "double opt-in" process (meaning that when your users enter their email address, they must confirm that email address by clicking on the confirmation link that is sent by Feedburner), you will need to setup the "From" address, the "Subject," and the "Body" of your initial confirmation message.

Email Branding – you can add your logo and change the font of your email messages here.

Delivery Options – set the time when you want your messages to be delivered.

We are done with the configuration for now. Go to "Edit Feed Details..." to collect some information for our plugin setup on the WordPress side.

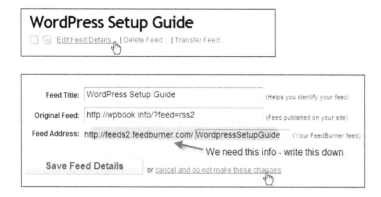

Now that we can see the details, record the information in the Feed Address. Our plugin won't work unless we have the URL exactly right. Once recorded, cancel any changes, or simply log out and head back to your WordPress administration page.

FD Feedburner Options

Once logged in to the admin page, find and click on the "Feedburner Configuration" link in the Plugins drop-down list on the sidebar.

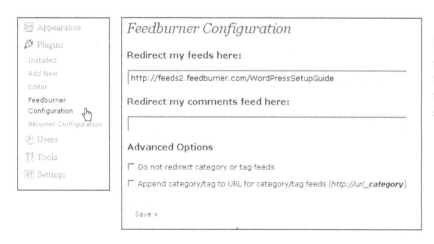

Enter the URL for your feed exactly as it appeared on the Feedburner site. Leave the comments feed field and the checkboxes blank.

> **NOTE:** *Comments are rarely subscribed to and are optional, you will need to burn another feed that is just for comments and enter that information here if you choose.*

Click "Save" to finish the plugin setup. From now on, when someone subscribes to your feed, they will automatically be directed to the correct URL and you will be able to track your subscribers.

Whew — that was a bit of work, but it will be totally worth it once you start logging in to Feedburner and reviewing your stats.

> *The FD Feedburner Plugin may require you to post a new article before it will redirect properly. Keep that in mind that if you are trying to view your RSS feeds and you get an error or "Page not found" message, simply post an article and that should fix it.*

THEMES

Every WordPress default installation comes with a default theme. The WordPress Default theme is very minimalist, but gets the job done, however, most of us will want to change our blog's look from the default. There are literally thousands of free and premium WordPress themes available for download. Simply do a search on the Internet for "WordPress themes" and you'll be bombarded with links to themes. You have to decide on a theme on your own. You can pay for premium themes, hire a designer to create a theme, or simply stay with the default. For our purposes, we are going to download and install a free theme.

Installing a New Theme

> *See Appendix A for version 2.8 changes to the Theme Installation.*

For demonstration purposes we are going to go through the installation of "Shades of Blue." Remember that the name of the theme you have chosen may be different. Our theme is available for download at *http://wordpress. org/extend/themes/shades-of-blue*. Simply click on the "Download" link and save the corresponding .zip file to your computer's hard drive (the Desktop is usually fine).

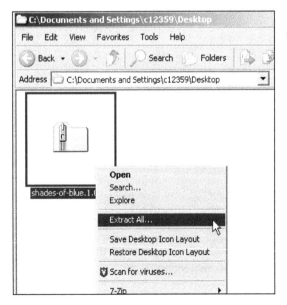

We need to unzip the folder to access the theme files.

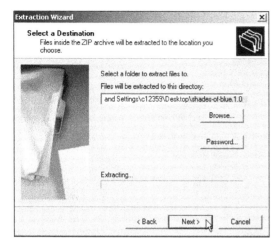

Extract the files to a location that you will remember.

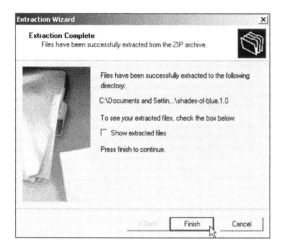

Now that the theme files have been extracted, there is usually a README.txt file or instructions file. Browse to the directory where the files were extracted to view any included documentation.

Most themes are simple and don't require any special considerations for installation so the install process is generally the same for all themes.

Theme files are located in a folder usually named the same as the theme. Most themes will extract files into a folder named for the version of the theme, and also a nested folder with the name of the theme. For our example, our Shades of Blue theme was extracted to \shades-of-blue.1.0\shades-of-blue.

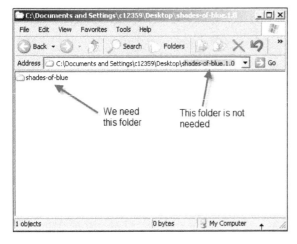

We need to upload just the "shades-of-blue" folder and not the "shades-of-blue.1.0" folder. You will find that most themes will create a similar folder structure when extracted.

Remember our handy little FTP program we used when we installed WordPress? Well, we need to bring that up again and upload the "shades-of-blue" folder to the proper directory.

In this case I have used WinSCP logged in to the *wpbook.info* site. I have browsed to the "shades-of-blue.1.0" folder on my computer. I also need to browse to the /wp-content/themes folder on the *wpbook.info* site.

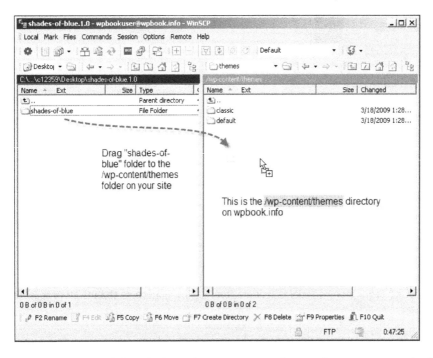

Drag the "shades-of-blue" folder to the /wp-content/themes directory to copy the files to the server.

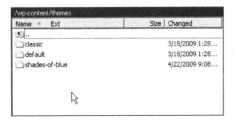

A new folder in the /wp-content/themes directory has been created. Now we need to activate that theme in our WordPress administration pages.

Find the themes options under the Appearance dropdown in the bottom sidebar of your WordPress administration dashboard.

You will notice that a new theme called Shades of Blue is now listed under Available Themes.

Click on the theme to preview it. A window should popup that will give you a glimpse of what the theme will look like.

Make sure to click on the "Activate" link located in the upper right corner of the preview window.

Your new theme is now active; visit your site to check out the new look.

NOTE: *Some themes have additional options that can be configured once installed. The instructions that are included in the download for the theme will detail the options and instruct you on how to configure them for your needs. Our theme is simple and does not require any additional options to be configured.*

Theme Widgets

See Appendix A for version 2.8 changes to Theme Widgets.

Theme widgets are an easy way for you to move and change the look of your blog by adding sections to the sidebars, footer, and sometimes the main content. With the use of a widget-ready theme, you have a lot of control over what information is displayed where.

> **NOTE:** *Most themes developed today are widget-ready, but you may find one that is not and therefore this functionality will not be available. Also, be aware that your theme's widgets may not have the same look, locations on the page, or content as the one's that come configured for Shades of Blue.*

For our new theme, the widgets are displayed on every page of our blog in the sidebar and footer.

These widgets are theme controlled and can be removed or changed at will. If you do not customize the widgets, the defaults will be used and as you can see, the default text in the footer widgets is not what we want to present. We need to change it.

To customize these, we need to navigate to the Appearance dropdown in the sidebar of the administration dashboard and click on the "Widgets" link.

On the right of the screen you can see all of the widget types that are available for use.

Recent Posts	Add	The most recent posts on your blog
Tag Cloud	Add	Your most used tags in cloud format
Categories	Add	A list or dropdown of categories
Text	Add	Arbitrary text or HTML
RSS	Add	Entries from any RSS or Atom feed
Recent Comments	Add	The most recent comments
Akismet	Add	

On the left of the screen are the positions that are available for placing widgets.

Recent Posts	Add	The most recent posts on your blog
Tag Cloud	Add	Your most used tags in cloud format
Categories	Add	A list or dropdown of categories
Text	Add	Arbitrary text or HTML
RSS	Add	Entries from any RSS or Atom feed
Recent Comments	Add	The most recent comments
Akismet	Add	

Our theme has 5 locations we can customize. Notice how we are using 0 widgets in each of the locations. That is because the theme has default widgets placed in these locations. As soon as you place/add a widget from the left to any of these locations, the defaults will be overridden.

I like how the theme has the Search, Categories, and a Text widget at the top of the sidebar. I want to duplicate that, but want to remove the Recent Posts, and Admin widgets.

Select the Sidebar widget from the dropdown menu and click on "Show."

Find the Search widget and click "Add." Next find the Categories widget and click "Add," then the Text widget and click "Add."

Make sure to click on "Save Changes." We have modified the Sidebar widget. Browse to the homepage of your blog to see the results.

Our sidebar got a lot shorter. Since I overrode the default widgets, only Search, Categories, and the Text widget are viewable. Our Text widget is a little empty, let's put a little "about me" text in there.

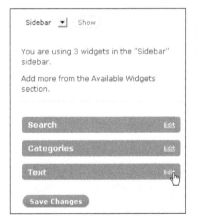

Back at your widgets administration page, find the Sidebar location and click on the Text widget's "Edit" link.

Add your copy to the text box and don't forget the title. Click "Done" and then don't forget to click the "Save Changes" button, too.

Let's see what your new Text widget looks like by browsing to your blog's home page.

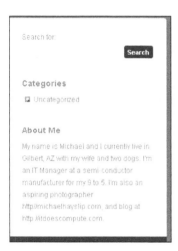

That looks a little better. Not so empty now. We still have some tweaks to do to the Text widget, like making the links clickable.

Back on our widgets management page, find the Text widget in the Sidebar location and click on the "Edit" link again.

I'm going to modify the text to include some clickable links. Here is an example of how to make a link clickable:

```
I'm also an aspiring photographer <a
href="http://michaelhayslip.com">michaelhayslip.
com</a>, and blog at <a href="http://
itdoescompute.com">itdoescompute.com</a>.
```

Notice how I have added the <a href> syntax to create the link. Now if we browse to the front page of our site, we can see how the links are clickable.

Using HTML is simple yet powerful and you can get crazy with customizations and functionality. If you are the type of person who wants to dive deeper into this for your blog, check out the resources for HTML at http://www.w3schools.com/html/.

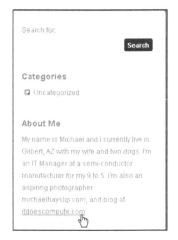

I filled in some of the blanks by adding a few more widgets to the sidebar and changing out the default footer widgets to complete the setup.

To change your widgets, simply switch to the different areas using the dropdown list and click on the "Show" button. Then place the widgets you want in those locations. Here is what I have chosen for the moment.

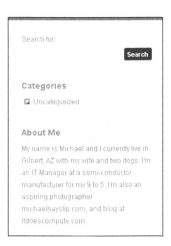

The Search, Categories, and a text widget I called "About Me" are visible in the top half of the sidebar.

I have also added the Archives and Links (also known as the Blogroll) widgets to the bottom half of the sidebar. You can change the positions of any of these simply by changing the order in the widgets administration page.

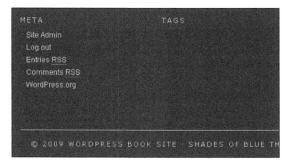

Footer locations 1 and 2 contain the Meta widget and the Tags widget. The Meta widget adds the Admin log-in link and some additional RSS links, while the Tags widget will display our blog's tags. Right now, we don't have any tags, but we'll get into creating some once we tackle the posting topic.

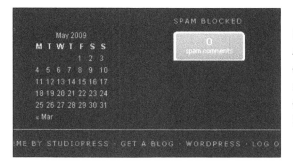

Footer locations 3 and 4 contain the Calendar and Akismet spam widgets. The Calendar will contain a clickable date based on your blog's posts and the Akismet spam widget will list how much spam has been caught. Not much to display for us now, but this will increase over time.

You can change the widgets and the positions of any of these widgets at any time. You're not stuck with it if you change your mind (and you probably will), so don't feel constrained or worry about this too much. It's all just aesthetics.

Now it's time to set the blog configuration aside and begin creating content. You will most likely come back to the configuration to make changes later.

CREATING CONTENT FOR YOUR WORD**PRESS** BLOG

WE ARE READY TO START WRITING CONTENT FOR THE BLOG. One of the most important details about your blog is the organization. Specifically we are talking about Pages, Categories, and Tags.

PAGES

Pages are fairly simple. The default WordPress installation has an "About" page already configured for us. Let's go find it and modify the content.

From your WordPress admin dashboard, find pages in the sidebar.

Once you click on the "Pages" link, you will see the current pages that are available to edit or delete. You can also create a new page if desired.

Click "Edit" under "About" to bring up the page editor.

The Write Panel

The Write Panel is where you will make changes to the content (the actual text, photos, or videos) on the page or post. Much of the workflow seen in creating a page will also be used to create posts. You will most often be using the Write Panel to create content — the more familiar you are with it, the faster you will be able to create content.

The preceding image is an example of my new "About" page. I've replaced the default text on the "About" page with my own. The editor is simple to use and is similar to most visual text editor programs. I even added a link to my other blog "It Does Compute" by clicking on the hyperlink icons. You may also add pictures.

Image Uploader/Editor

Clicking on the "Add an Image" icon brings up the Image Uploader/Editor.

I've chosen an image from my computer by clicking on "Select Files." The image was then uploaded to my WordPress hosting server and I added details as seen above. I chose to show only the thumbnail size of 150x150 for this example.

Custom Fields

How you use the Custom Fields section will depend on your blog's theme and is generally used for posts instead of pages. See your theme's README or documentation to determine when/if/how to use custom fields. We won't need a custom field for our "About" page, so I'm leaving it blank.

Discussion

I've disabled comments for the "About" page. I just simply want to relay the information and don't need the interaction of comments for this page. Pings are also disabled. Since I don't want comments, I also don't want to visually indicate (in the comments section) who has linked back to my page. Click on the "trackbacks and pingbacks" link to learn more about what this means.

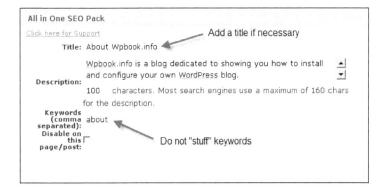

Since we installed the All in One SEO Pack plugin, we can add some additional information to help search engines like Google and Yahoo index our page. The Title field can be used if your page or post title is not very detailed. For us, "About" is not very exciting. I have changed it to "About Wpbook.info." The description field can also be filled out to include some additional information. The Keyword field is used to specify the "keywords" for this page. Do not "stuff" every possible keyword into this field. Search engines are smart about keywords and no longer put as much weight into your page ranking based on keywords. Use keywords lightly as "stuffing" can hinder your ranking.

We have managed to modify our "About" page. We'll create a contact info page from scratch.

Add a New Page

Click on the "Add New" link under Pages in the sidebar.

You will need to choose your title carefully. Many themes will display page titles as part of the site navigation. We have chosen "Contact" as our title and added a few details in the visual editor.

We are disabling comments and pings for this page. Also we have added a few details in the All in One SEO Pack fields.

The Attributes widget will be visible on the right. The dropdown allows you to nest this page under another (already created) page. We'll leave this "Contact" page at the top level. I did modify the order of the page, as I want to ensure that it appears after the "About" page in the navigation. Experiment with this if your navigation is not ordered how you would like it.

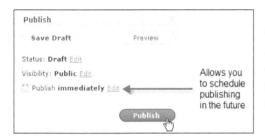

When your page editing is complete, you can publish. Clicking on the "Preview" button will open a new tab or window where you can view the newly created page without making it public. You can also schedule the page to go live for sometime in the future. Click publish to make the page live.

You should get a confirmation that the page has been published. If we browse to the new page, we can see that the navigation has also been updated.

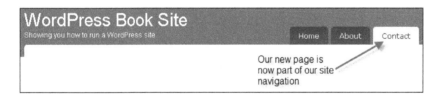

We have now created new content for our site. A new page can easily be created in a few simple steps. Pages should be thought of as static content because pages don't change very often. Once we create a page, we rarely go back to it unless the information contained within the page (phone number, address, etc.) needs updating.

We are now ready to move into creating our dynamic content — our posts or articles. Posts are a lot like pages in the way that you create them. They use the same visual editor, custom fields, comment system, and publishing methods. But before we can write posts, we will need to understand how to categorize them. For that, we need to explain Categories and Tags.

CATEGORIES AND TAGS

Within your blog you have two ways to sort and catalog posts: categories and tags.

Categories

Categories are the broadest divisions and cover the overall themes of your blog. The ideal number of categories is 3 to 8. If you need more than 8 categories, your choices may be too specific. Remember that categories are your main themes not the details.

Tags

Tags subdivide the content within your categories into finer sections. Categories give visitors a wide-angle view of your blog and tags help users to sort those broad areas into posts related to a specific topic or subject. You will have more tags than categories but that's not a license to go crazy. If you find yourself adding new tags frequently, the subject matter of your posts has probably become too broad or unrelated to your main topic.

How do I choose categories and tags?

If you are having trouble picking your categories and tags, you can follow the steps below to help you narrow down the list.

Step 1: Start broad and brainstorm

Sit down with a fresh pad of Post-it® notes and jot down any topics you would like to write about. (Remember that these will eventually be your tags and categories, so try to limit your choices to one- or two-word phrases.) At this point, the more ideas the better so write down anything that comes to mind. If you find yourself running out of ideas, ask yourself a few questions:

1. What questions are my customers always asking me?
2. What products or services are at the core of my business?
3. What are common mistakes related to my business or industry?

Repeat this process over several days or a week. Ask colleagues, friends, and family to describe what they think you do. Add any new words to your Post-it stack. After a week, you should have quite a list of possible tags and categories—now it's time to sort them.

Step 2: Cluster related items together

Find a large blank wall in your home or office and stick your Post-its with your word ideas on it. Don't try to sort or group them—just stick them to the wall so you can see them all at once. As you post them, read each one and eliminate any that jump out to you as duds. If you're not sure, stick it to the wall and sort it later.

Once you have them all on the wall, look over the words and start clustering related items together. Try to get your notes sorted into 3 to 8 big chunks. If you have something that just doesn't fit, decide if it truly belongs. Chances are it is out of topic and should be eliminated. As you sort, eliminate any more words that you think are duds. Once you have everything sorted into 3 to 8 large groups, it's time to choose your categories and tags.

Step 3: Choose categories and tags

Read through each of the clusters one at a time and write down the common word or phrase that ties them together into the categories column of this worksheet. The word or phrase should be 1 to 2 words. If you can't condense it down, try something else. Use a thesaurus to find related words if you get stuck. Once you do this for each cluster, you will have your list of categories.

Now take each cluster off the wall one at a time and write those words in the tags column of this worksheet. As you write eliminate any that are duplicates or don't have a strong impact. Don't be afraid to weed things out—you want the strongest possible set of tags. You can always add new ones later if they are needed. Once you've done this with each cluster, you will have a list of tags for your blog.

Keyword and category worksheet

CATEGORIES	TAGS
Remember: No more than 8 categories!	

NOTE: *Categories are often used to break up the navigation in your blog's theme via a menu system. You will often find that a blog will group articles by topic (that topic is determined from the post's category).*

There are two methods to adding Categories and Tags. You can add them up front (before creating content), or add them on the fly (as you create content). It is recommended to add your Categories and Tags up front. By adding them before you create content, you will have an easier time keeping your blog focused.

For our *wpbook.info* blog, we will use the following Categories:

- Howto
    - Widgets
    - Posts
- Themes
- Customization
- SEO
- Blog Promotion

> *Notice my intent to place "Widgets" and "Posts" as children of the "Howto" category.*

And the following tags:

- Blogging
- Tips
- HTML
- Custom code
- Media
- Video
- Tools
- Software
- Security
- Possibly more if the topic requires.

Let's add these now.

In the Dashboard, find the Posts dropdown and click on the "Categories" link.

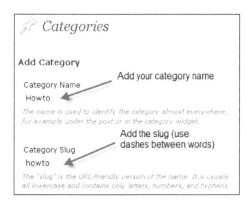

Add the category name as you want it to appear on the site. Spaces are allowed for Category Name; however, Category Slug should not have spaces. If you have a multiple word category, use dashes between the words to keep it one continuous word. For example, the Category Slug for "Blog Promotion" will be "blog-promotion."

The Category Parent is used to sub-categorize content. This is usually seen in the navigation of your blog. If you find that your content can be subdivided, feel free to add categories as child categories. For now, I have "Widgets" and "Posts" as children of the "Howto" category.

Click the "Add Category" button to continue. Repeat the process for each category you will add.

Name	Description	Slug	Posts
Howto — Posts Edit	Quick Edit	Delete		posts	0
Howto — Widgets		widgets	0
Blog Promotion		blog-promotion	0
SEO		seo	0
Customization		customization	0
Themes		themes	0
Howto		howto	0
Uncategorized		uncategorized	1
Name	Description	Slug	Posts

Your categories list will contain links to "Edit/Quick Edit" and "Delete" each category. If you feel that you have made a mistake, you can edit the category, or simply delete it. Any content assigned to a deleted category will default to Uncategorized.

We need to add Tags now. Find the "Tags" link under the Posts sidebar in the dashboard.

Adding Tags is very similar to adding Categories. Simply enter the Tag names as you want them to appear on the site, add a slug, and click the "Add Tag" button.

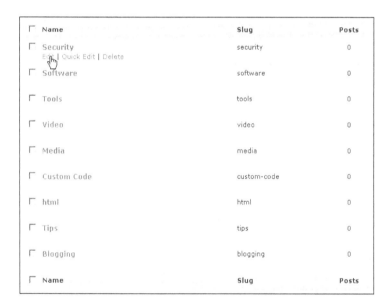

Name	Slug	Posts
Security	security	0
Edit	Quick Edit	Delete		
Software	software	0
Tools	tools	0
Video	video	0
Media	media	0
Custom Code	custom-code	0
html	html	0
Tips	tips	0
Blogging	blogging	0
Name	Slug	Posts

Your Tag list will have the same "Edit/Quick Edit" and "Delete" links as the Categories list. Deleting a Tag simply removes it from any tagged posts; it will not delete the post associated with the Tag.

POSTS

Posts (also known as articles) are the bread and butter of your site. Posts are constantly being added to your site to keep the information fresh. The more dynamic your blog, the more readers you will potentially have, and the more visible you will become to search engines.

The "Post" interface is very similar to the "Pages" interface and should be somewhat familiar by now, however, there are a couple of additional things to note.

Find and click on the "Add New" link under the Posts dropdown in the sidebar of the dashboard.

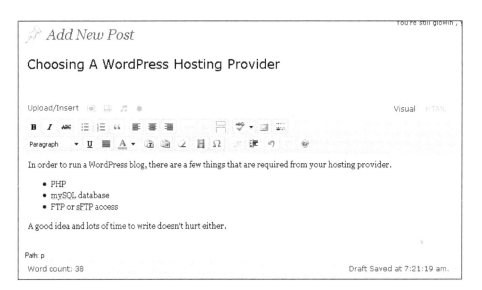

Enter the content of the Post in the Write panel. The title of our Post will also be the title of the web page for the article (if that is confusing, don't worry, I'll show you a bit later what this means). You'll also notice that I chose to use bullets to format some of my information. The Write Panel has many formatting choices. Be sure to explore the interface as you write your content.

NOTE: *The information provided in these sample posts is for demonstration purposes only. I just needed a minimum amount of content to provide examples as we discuss the process.*

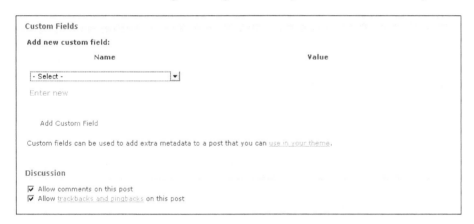

The Excerpt field is not required in this theme, but if it were, you would simple add something that would tease folks. Most people just copy and paste from the first paragraph of the Post and that is perfectly acceptable.

The Send Trackbacks field is for legacy blogs. This is generally left blank. If your post contains a link back to another blog, that blog will normally detect that automatically.

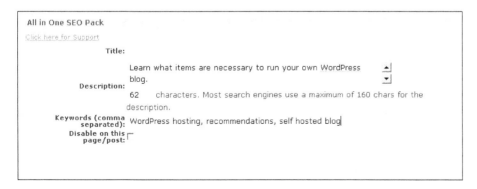

We don't have a need for Custom Fields, as our blog's theme does not use them.

We do want to allow others to comment and ping our post. This encourages interaction from readers and other bloggers.

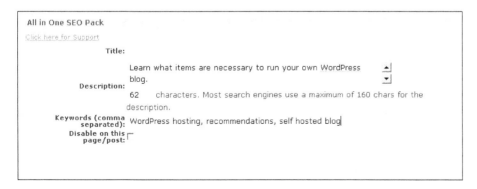

If you have changed the permalinks as described earlier in the "Configuring Your Wordpress Blog" section, you will notice that all of your page titles will reflect your post's title. The Title of my post as I want it to appear in search engines and on the webpage title can be changed using the Title field. You should use this if your need to add information to the title to make it more search engine friendly. Most of the time, it will be left blank.

The Description field should contain a few words about the post's content. This information can sometimes be displayed on search engines and depending on what you write here, you can potentially turn off visitors if the information is not relevant to what they need. So keep it brief so that those who are doing a search will have to click through to the site to read the full content.

Again, just like pages, we also have keywords. Keep them brief and relevant. Don't go wild.

The rest of the workflow for a Post is found on the right sidebar. We are looking for Tags and Categories.

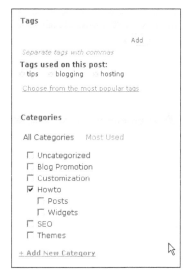

Remember our list of tags from the previous exercise? Let's pick a couple of relevant tags and add a new one while we are at it. I chose to use "tips," "blogging," and added a new tag called "hosting." Adding a new tag is easy to do, and as long as it is relevant to the topic, you are certainly free to add a new tag now and then. If your topic is about "Health Food Myths," then don't tag anything "Ford Trucks" or "HDTV." Those tags are not relevant in any way to your article (even if you mention "Ford Trucks" or "HDTV" in your article).

The current list of categories is visible in the Categories widget. These are the categories we decided on earlier and should try to place each post into a category. We have chosen the "Howto" category for this article.

NOTE: *See how the "Posts" and "Widgets" categories are indented a bit to show their child relationship to the "Howto" category.*

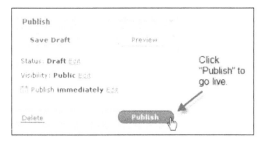

You can now publish the article. Clicking the "Publish" button will allow the post to show up on the blog.

You can now view the post by clicking on the "View post" link, or by simply browsing to your blog's URL.

The Finished Post

If we browse to the front page of our site, we can see how the newly published article has affected the blog.

Notice that the first article/post that appears is our most recent. The Hello World article is no longer at the top of the page. Our article also contains a few extra links at the bottom that will help readers find more related articles. This is why it is important to try to add articles to already existing categories and tags.

Categories and Tags

The Categories and Tags have also changed.

Take a look at the sidebar widgets. We can see that a new category has been added to the Categories list. You will continue to populate this widget automatically as you add posts to the rest of your categories.

Our "Tags" widget on the footer has also changed. We can now see that we have used three tags and if you hover over the tags with your mouse you can learn how many articles are tagged with that name (this function is theme dependant, but most do this).

We have a couple of more details to look at in the post itself.

The Post Page

We can certainly see the post on the blog's front page. It is the first in the list. I also want to show you that each post has a unique link. Clicking on the title of the post will bring up its individual page.

Click on the post's title to view just the single article alone.

Since we have changed the Permalink structure (as described in the "Configuring your WordPress Blog" chapter), we now have a URL that reflects our post's topic. We can also see that the page title that appears at the top of the browser also shows the name of the post. If we needed to change the page title as it appeared at the top of the browser, we would modify it using the "All in One SEO" plugin as we wrote the article.

Adding Photos

I like the post I just created, but how about adding a photo to make it stand out a bit.

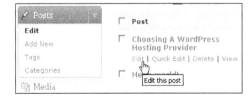

Go back to the Posts dropdown and click on the "Edit" link, then find the article we just created and click on its "Edit" link.

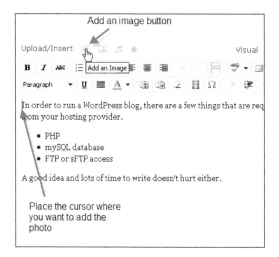

Once the editor for the post appears, you will need to place the cursor where you would like the photo to appear and click on the "Add an Image" button.

Choose the photo from your computer by using the "Select Files" button. Once the file is uploaded by the wizard, you can then modify the parameters such as Title, Caption, and Description.

You should also decide what will happen when readers click on the photo by modifying the Link URL field. If you click the "None" button, the photo will not link to anything. Selecting the "File URL" button will tell WordPress to open a new window with the full sized image displayed. The "Post URL" button will simply link back to the current post.

I want to show a larger version of the image when readers click on the photo, so I click on the "File URL" button to populate the Link URL field.

I have also chosen to show the thumbnail version of the photo and align it to the left of the post.

Be sure to click the "Insert into Post" button to complete the task.

The image is now added to the post. It looks a bit large at 150x150. I can modify the size by clicking on the image. This will allow me to see the "Edit Image" and "Delete Image" icons. Click on the "Edit Image" icon.

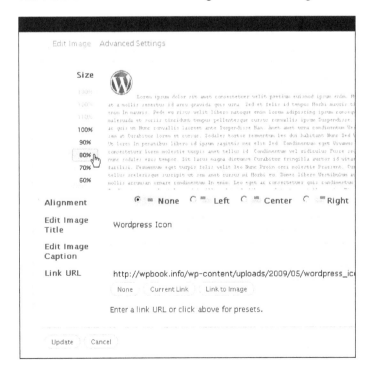

I elected to reduce the size to 80% and set the alignment to "None" (meaning the image will be on a line by itself). Click the "Update" button to make the change.

Once you are satisfied with the look, you can publish.

Click the "Update Post" button located on the right sidebar to make the changes live.

We now need to move on to how to manage your comments.

Post Comments

Because we want interaction with our readers, we allow readers to comment. The comment form will become visible on the individual post's page. You will need to click on the Post's title to see it.

Find the comment form at the bottom of the post.

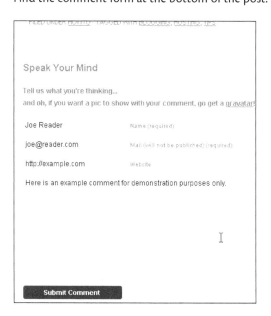

After Joe Reader hits the submit button his comment can only be seen by him as it is awaiting moderation.

To help curb spam, we chose to allow comments to appear only if the comment author had a previously approved comment. I have never approved a comment from Joe Reader, so if I want his comment to appear on the site, I will have to approve it.

But how will I know that a comment is awaiting approval? I can simple check my email, or log into the administration dashboard to find out.

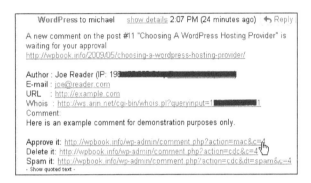

Here is an example of an email notification about a recent comment that is now awaiting approval. I can click on the "Approve," "Delete," or "Spam" links which will take me to the comment administration page where I can confirm the action I want to take.

If we choose, we can also log into the administration dashboard and find the "Recent Comments" widget.

We can see that our friend Joe Reader's comment is listed here. If I hover over his comment I will see a list of available tasks (Approve, Edit, Reply, Spam, or Delete). This method of approval works great if you only have a handful of comments. What if you need to make a bunch of comment approvals at once? There is an easier way.

2 comments are awaiting approval

Find the top sidebar in the administration dashboard and you will notice that the "Comments" link will have an annotated number in a small circle. The number indicates how many comments are waiting to be approved. If we click on the "Comments" link, we can take action on the comments administration page.

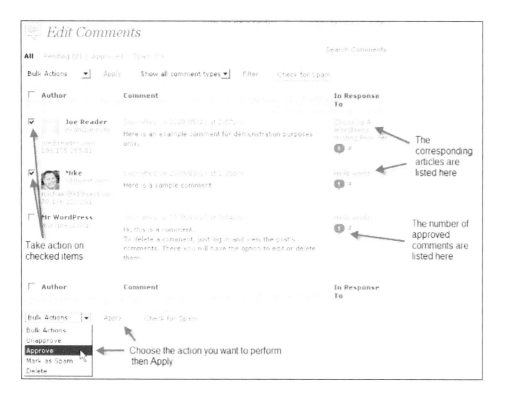

The comments administration page is full of useful information. The top of the page will list the number of comments that are currently pending, approved, or marked as spam. Comments awaiting approval are highlighted.

We can check multiple comments and choose to do a bulk action on them by choosing the drop-down menu. Be sure to click the "Apply" button to make the changes take effect.

Approved Comments

Once you have approved a comment, it will become visible by all users. We can view the post in our browser to see the updates.

Choosing A WordPress Hosting Provider

Posted by Michael Hayslip on Tuesday, May 19, 2009 · 1 Comment

In order to run a WordPress blog, there are a few things that are required

Comments

One Response to "Choosing A WordPress Hosting Provider"

Joe Reader says:
May 20, 2009 at 2:07 pm

Here is an example comment for demonstration purposes only

Our article's comment count has been updated (some themes will not display this information) and we can now see that Joe Reader's comment is no longer being held for approval.

Okay. That's it! You're ready to go. Sure there are a few hundred little tweaks you can do along the way to customize your blog, but the hard part is now over. Keep posting and creating content.

WORD**PRESS**
BLOG
MAINTENANCE

YOUR BLOG'S MAINTENANCE IS FAIRLY SIMPLE. Here are a few things you need to keep up on.

PLUGIN UPDATES

You need to keep on top of your plugin versions. Often new features and security fixes are released that can benefit our WordPress installation.

A notification bubble appears on the sidebar when a plugin upgrade is available.

Click on the "Plugin" link to review the list of plugins and do an automatic upgrade.

The All in One SEO Pack is out of date. Click on "upgrade automatically" to start the upgrade.

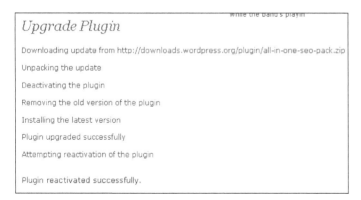

The upgrade should go through the above steps in less than 20 seconds (depending on your connection speed). If you go back to the Plugins administration page, you will now see the updated version listed.

BLOG VERSION UPGRADES

See Appendix A for version 2.8 changes to the Upgrade Process.

The WordPress team is constantly making improvements to the WordPress platform. Keep an eye out in your dashboard for an upgrade notification.

Version 2.7.1 gives you the option of upgrading "automatically." I often choose to do an automatic upgrade because it is easy and fast. Make sure you do a backup of the database first (which you can do using the WP-DB-Backup plugin we installed).

Once you click the "Please update now" link, you will be able to change some parameters.

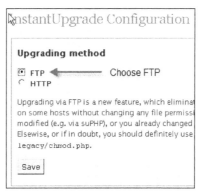

Ensure that FTP is used as the transfer method since it is more reliable.

Enter your site FTP password and click the "Upgrade my Word-Press!" button.

InstantUpgrade

Performing Upgrade ...

- **Upgrade method: FTP.**
- Connecting to the FTP server ...
- Login to FTP server.
- Setting mode to automatic ASCII detection.
- Setting mode to PASV.
- Downloading WordPress installation package ...
- Downloading file http://wordpress.org/latest.zip was successful. Filesize: 1853086 bytes.
- Extracting WordPress package latest.zip ...
- Removing old files ...
- Inserting new files ...
- Wiping out temporary files ...
- Running upgrade script of new WordPress version ...

Result:
Everything went smooth. Have fun with your new WordPress version!

In about 30 seconds you should see "Upgrade complete!" If you have been keeping up with your blog's plugin upgrades, this process should go really smoothly.

> **NOTE:** *Please remember to read the version upgrade notes and do a little research on any known issues or problems with a newly released version of WordPress. You don't have to upgrade immediately, and in fact should wait a few weeks to let others "burn-in" the latest version before you dive in.*

SPAM CONTAINMENT

Spam is a nuisance. Please be sure to review your comments on a regular basis and mark items as spam whenever you can. The more Akismet is aware of what to look for, the easier it will be it to catch it before it gets posted. If you choose to let anybody comment without having a previously approved comment, this is especially important. Don't let it get out of hand or your readers will get annoyed and stop visiting.

WORD**PRESS** BLOG PROMOTION

NOW THAT YOU HAVE A BLOG UP AND RUNNING and know how to publish and edit your posts, it's time to think about blog promotion. The most important aspect to having a successful blog is to have good content. You can promote your blog until you are blue in the face, but if nobody cares about your content, your repeat readers will be non-existent.

SUBMITTING TO SEARCH ENGINES

The first step in blog promotion is to submit your site to Google. Google will index your site so that our pages appear in search queries by *google.com* users. To ensure that Google has the right information, use the free Webmaster Tools.

Using your browser go to *http://www. google.com/webmasters*.

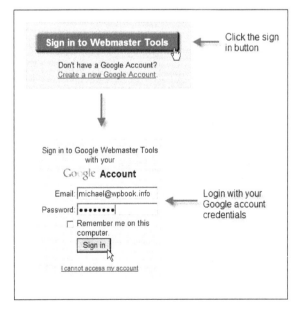

The account information is the same username and password used when you setup your Feedburner account. Feedburner is a Google product, and therefore you can use the same username and password to access all your Google data.

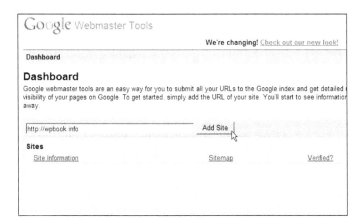

Once you have finished logging in you should see the Webmaster Tools Dashboard. Enter your site's URL and click the "Add Site" button.

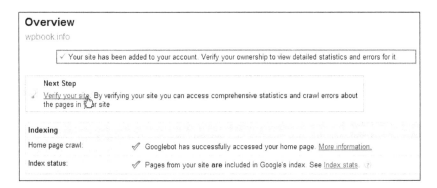

Google will attempt to contact your website. If everything works out, you should see the green checkboxes and a "Next Step" box.

We need to let Google know that we own the site we have just submitted, so click on the "Verify your site" URL to continue.

The verify process can be done in two ways. Upload an HTML file to your website, or add a META tag to your website's homepage. I prefer to use the META tag method because I can use my web browser to complete the verification tasks and don't need to open another program (text editor, FTP) to finish verification.

Choose the "Add meta tag" option and you should see some additional text displayed. Copy this text to your clipboard.

Your site now needs to be updated to include this META tag. Google will attempt to visit the homepage of your website and detect whether this tag exists. You need to install the META tag code on your blog. You will do this by modifying one of the theme files. To do this you need to get back into your WordPress administration dashboard.

Once you are logged in to the dashboard, find the Appearance dropdown in the sidebar and click the "Editor" link.

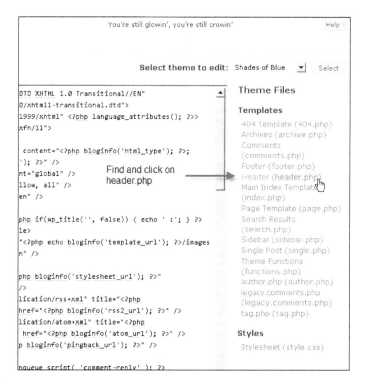

Once you have opened the theme editor you will need to find your theme's *"header.php"* file. Click on it to make it the active file to be edited.

Header (header.php)   Select theme to edit:

```
<!DOCTYPE html PUBLIC "-//W3C//DTD XHTML 1.0 Transitional//EN" "http://www.w3.org
/TR/xhtml1/DTD/xhtml1-transitional.dtd">
<html xmlns="http://www.w3.org/1999/xhtml" <?php language_attributes(); ?>>
<head profile="http://gmpg.org/xfn/11">

<meta http-equiv="Content-Type" content="<?php bloginfo('html_type'); ?>;
charset=<?php bloginfo('charset'); ?>" />
<meta name="distribution" content="global" />
<meta name="robots" content="follow, all" />
<meta name="language" content="en" />            ← Paste after the last meta tag
<meta name="verify-v1" content="si▮▮▮▮▮▮▮▮▮▮▮▮▮▮▮CI=" />

<title><?php wp_title(''); ?><?php if(wp_title('', false)) { echo ' :'; } ?>
<?php bloginfo('name'); ?></title>
<link rel="Shortcut Icon" href="<?php echo bloginfo('template_url'); ?>/images
/favicon.ico" type="image/x-icon" />

<link rel="stylesheet" href="<?php bloginfo('stylesheet_url'); ?>"
type="text/css" media="screen" />
<link rel="alternate" type="application/rss+xml" title="<?php bloginfo('name');
?> RSS Feed" href="<?php bloginfo('rss2_url'); ?>" />
<link rel="alternate" type="application/atom+xml" title="<?php bloginfo('name');
?> Atom Feed" href="<?php bloginfo('atom_url'); ?>" />
<link rel="pingback" href="<?php bloginfo('pingback_url'); ?>" />

<?php if ( is_singular() ) wp_enqueue_script( 'comment-reply' ); ?>
```

(Update File)

Find the last "<meta>" tag that is currently in the file and paste your Google "<meta>" tag code right after it. Then click "Update File" to make the changes take effect.

Now go back to your webmaster account to finish the process.

Click the "Verify" button to begin verification.

After a few seconds a "successfully verified" message should appear along with a warning that "You have not submitted any Sitemaps." Your next step is to tell Google where your sitemap is located.

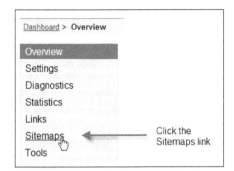

Find and click on the "Sitemaps" link on the left side of the Google Webmaster Tools Dashboard.

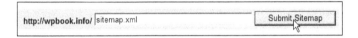

If you recall, we added a Google XML Sitemaps plugin to the blog earlier and generated a sitemap using the plugin. The default sitemap that is generated by the plugin is called *"sitemap.xml."* Enter *"sitemap.xml"* in the field and click one "Submit Sitemap."

After a few seconds of Google churning away, you should see a success page.

You're done. Check back on your Webmaster Tools account every so often to view the reports and recommendations for making your site more search engine friendly. Check out your Settings and Diagnostics pages — Google includes lots of "Learn more" links to help you understand what you are looking at or changing.

You have now finished submitting your site to Google. You may also want to consider submitting your *"sitemap.xml"* file to other search engines like MSN Search, *Ask.com*, and *Yahoo.com*. This is not required, but may help you become visible to users who don't regularly use Google, but some other search engine. See the help documentation on your Google XML Sitemaps plugin to learn more.

TRACKING STATISTICS

If you start to promote your blog, how will you know if your efforts are successful? You need to track statistics.

Tracking website statistics (from now on abbreviated as "stats") helps analyze your website's performance and gives you a bit of insight into the type of visitors you are receiving.

Stats include useful information like which sites referred readers to you, the geographic location of your readers, what content is most/least popular, etc. We will show you how to install free tracking software from "Google" that records all of this information plus much, much more.

Google Analytics

To get started with Google Analytics, you first need login to the Analytics site with your Google account information. The account information is the same username and password used when you setup your Feedburner account. Feedburner is a Google product, and therefore you can use the same username and password to access all of your Google data.

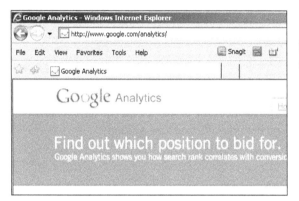

Browse to the Google analytics web site at *http://www.google.com/analytics*.

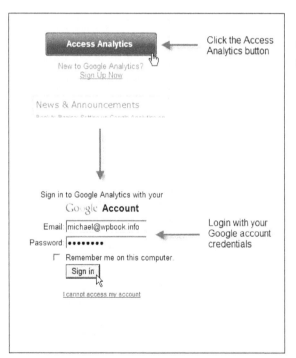

Click the "Access Analytics" button and then enter the credentials for your Google account.

If you have never setup analytics, you will see the "Sign up >>" button.

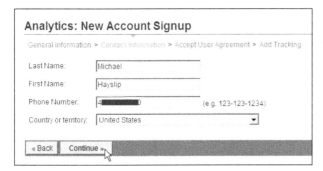

Enter the information for your site and click "Continue >>."

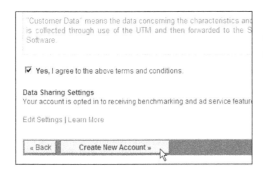

Make sure to check the box to accept the terms and conditions and then click "Create New Account >>."

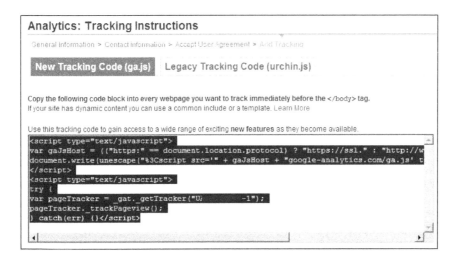

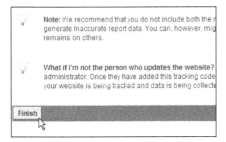

The screen that appears will contain your tracking code. You should copy this code to your clipboard before clicking the "Finish" button.

Now that you have created the account, you need to install the tracking code on your blog. You will do this by modifying one of the theme files. To do this you need to get back in to your WordPress administration dashboard.

Once you are logged in to the dashboard, find the Appearance dropdown in the sidebar and click the "Editor" link.

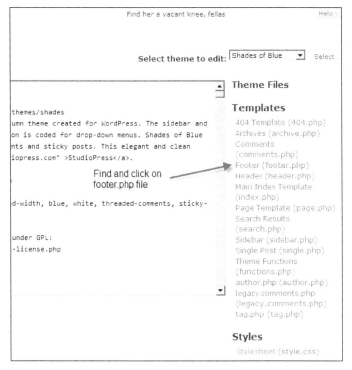

Once you have opened the theme editor you will need to find your theme's *"footer. php"* file. Click on it to make it the active file to be edited.

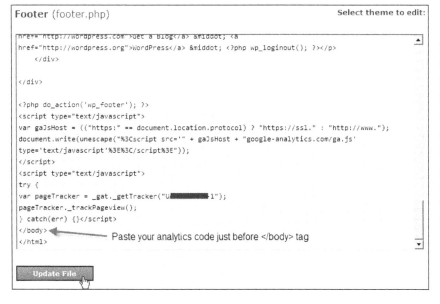

Scroll to the bottom of the file *(footer.php)*, and paste the tracking code into the line just before the "</body>" tag and click the "Update File" button. Since *"footer. php"* is used on all pages of your WordPress site, Google will be able to track stats for all of your pages/posts.

We need to go back to the analytics account to finish the process.

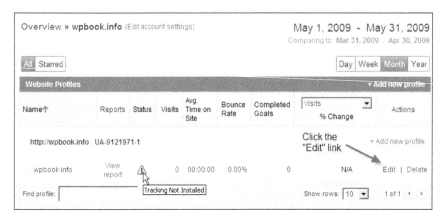

You should be at the "Overview" screen of your analytics account. You may notice that a warning triangle is displayed next to your site's name. This means that you haven't yet told Google to scan your site for the analytics code.

Click on the "Edit" link for your site's profile.

You can see that Google is reporting that tracking is not installed. If we click the "Check Status" link, Google will attempt to scan for the tracking code on your WordPress site.

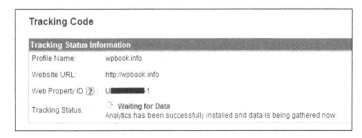

If all worked as planned you should see that analytics has been successfully installed.

NOTE: *As of this writing Google analytics does not display data in real time. You will see that the "Waiting for Data" display will remain until Google has collected enough data to report on. Data in the analytics display is usually 24 hours old.*

If you click on the Google icon or the "Analytics Settings" link at the top left corner of the page, the main analytics page is displayed.

You can then see that the icon has changed from a triangle to a clock formation. This icon indicates that Google is waiting for enough data to produce reports. Once enough data has been collected, the icon will change to a green check mark.

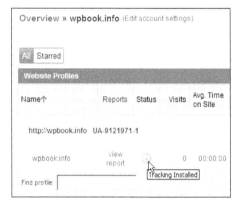

If you click on the "View report" link you will see the report with zero data at this point. Come back tomorrow and check the report.

Analytics is a very powerful tool for collecting web site stats. Using and understanding the analytics data is beyond the scope of this book. Google provides tons of information on how to analyze your data in their help documents. Some of the canned reports are easy to understand, so don't feel like you have to take a course to get value out of the data. You can get as detailed as you wish, if you wish.

The point of all this is to get readers. Now that tracking has been installed, your campaign to get more readers can be measured. So how do you let people know your blog exists? Join communities and get some friends.

JOINING COMMUNITIES

Why join a community? Joining a community is a good way to publicize your blog's URL. The more your URL shows up in directory listings, the more traffic is generated. Think of this as marketing for your blog.

Community Guidelines

Here are few guidelines for joining a community. These are by no means set in stone. If you feel that deviating from these guidelines works best for you, go for it.

Have enough content to keep readers interested. There is nothing more disappointing than to go to someone's blog and find they only have one post. Try to write five good posts before you start to promote. If there is interest in what you are writing, viewers may stick around and read your other articles as well as subscribe to your blog (remember RSS?).

Use a pleasing avatar. The best avatar is a photo of you. Something "Rated G" is preferred (no party pics or crazy poses). Sometimes an avatar that displays your logo or your product can work. Be careful when choosing your avatar as you don't want you/your account to be associated with "shameless promotion." That turns people off. Being yourself usually works best.

Don't just promote your own stuff. As you join these communities, keep in mind that you should try to participate as much as possible. Not only are you trying to promote your blog, but you are trying to connect with others as well. The value of connections is important because if you scratch someone else's back, they may scratch yours. Help promote someone's great blog post, and they may return the favor.

Have something good to share. If this is your everyday article that took you all of five minutes to write and there are 100 other articles out there just like it, don't try to promote the article; only promote your best stuff.

Here is a list of some of the more popular communities to get you started.

StumbleUpon

Stumbleupon is a great service for discovering new websites and great content. The StumbleUpon community is made up of users who help each other discover new sites by sharing and reviewing interesting articles, posts, pages, news items, etc. I don't need to get into a lot of detail as they explain it pretty well on their "About Us" page. Please visit *http://www.stumbleupon.com/aboutus/* to learn more about the service and to sign up.

Here is an example of Stumbling onto a site. Let's assume you have the StumbleUpon browser toolbar already installed (which you can get when you sign up) and you have told StumbleUpon what interests you.

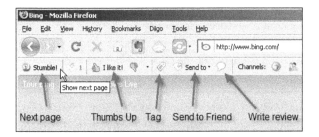

The toolbar includes a "Stumble!" button which when pressed, will randomly pick a new page to display for you that matches the categories you indicated you were interested in. Once you check out the content on the page, you have a few options.

Clicking "I like it!" will help move it up in popularity as well as help StumbeUpon better understand your preferences (the more you participate the better this algorithm gets). Clicking the thumbs down link will slow down the popularity ranking. Lots of thumbs downs from many uses will most likely kill the link. Meaning StumbleUpon will recognize that nobody is interested in the page's content and will stop sending people there. You can tag the page, which helps StumbleUpon place the content in the right categories. You can also send the article to a friend (if you have made any in the StumbleUpon community), or write a review.

StumbleUpon is a great tool for a few reasons:

- StumbleUpon is all about discovery, so it's fun. If you're into web design, what better way to find new articles, topics, or trends than by user submitted content.
- It can generate a lot of traffic. Depending on the number of "Thumbs Ups," the article's popularity can increase. You can receive upwards of 60,000 visits in a day for something that gets really popular.
- The traffic keeps coming. StumbleUpon is still sending traffic to one of my articles over a year later.
- StumbleUpon learns about your interests and sends you to the sites in which you are most likely interested which helps you to easily connect with other StumbleUpon users and make friends.

Befriending another StumbleUpon user is easy. You can find others in your neighborhood (geographic location), in your niche, or who have your interests, and ask them to be a friend. Once you have friends, you can submit content to StumbleUpon and ask your friends to "Thumbs Up" or review your submitted article. Maybe they'll send you their articles someday, too. You can return the favor.

NOTE: *StumbleUpon is smart. Submitting content from your blog too often, or not participating will backfire on you. There are countless blog posts about users submitting content and not getting any traction. They have been flagged and are no longer considered "organic" users. They are shameless promoters and not very popular.*

There's one more really great reason that StumbleUpon is one of my favorites — campaigns. Campaigns are a super easy way to get inexpensive traffic to your site. Since the whole point of StumbleUpon is to target content to a specific user's interests, your campaign is no different.

Each visit to your page through the use of StumbleUpon costs you 5 cents. If you decide to buy a $5 campaign, it gets you 100 visits guaranteed. If those users "Thumbs Up" the page, that can generate even more visits. Campaigns are an inexpensive way to get feedback on your content. StumbleUpon lets you see reports of how many "Thumbs Up" and "Thumbs Down" clicks your page received, as well as read the reviews that users may have submitted.

What are you waiting for? Go get an account and start stumbling.

BlogCatalog

Similar to StumbleUpon, BlogCatalog allows you to create a profile and add friends. BlogCatalog also lists your blog in their directory under the blog's niche. Your blog will need to be submitted and reviewed by the Blog-Catalog staff before they will allow it to be listed in the directory.

BlogCatalog is really effective in the "Community" aspect of blogging. There are discussion groups on just about any blogging topic. You can join a group to help promote blogs in your niche, or just join a discussion on how to get more comments on your posts. Visit other user's blogs, and they may return the favor and even give your site a nice review. Send out broadcast messages to your BlogCatalog friends and community members to promote your posts.

MyBlogLog

MyBlogLog.com is a Yahoo service and is very similar to BlogCatalog. MyBlogLog also offers some free website stats. You'll also have to have the site approved before you start using the service. They both have similar features, but it's wise to sign up for both to get the most out of your promotion efforts.

Digg

Digg.com is another way to get your content viewed. If an article that is submitted to *Digg.com* makes it to the front page of *Digg.com,* you could potentially receive tons of traffic. Set up an account and start poking around on the *Digg.com* site.

You'll see articles throughout the site that look similar to the one above. After you read the content, you can "digg" the article and help it gain popularity. You can submit your own content and make friends, too. Digg is a lot of fun. Some of the articles are very interesting and if you're also using StumbleUpon, you can "Thumbs Up" anything you have "Dugg." This will make a lot of sense once you start "stumbling" and "digging."

Forums and Other Blogs

Just because you have a blog, doesn't mean you should ignore other blogs. Bloggers want to interact with other bloggers (that is one reason why BlogCatalog and MyBlogLog are so popular). Find other blogs in your niche and visit and comment on them regularly.

Most blogging/commenting systems allow you to leave a link back to your site (usually when someone clicks on your name, it links back to your site). If you leave a comment on a popular blog, this can potentially lead to some significant traffic by other readers of that blog. But a comment that says nothing does more harm than good. When I say "says nothing," I'm referring to those comments like "Nice post — thx" or "Keep it up." Those comments don't add anything to the conversation and can even be considered as spam. If you sincerely want the reader to "keep it up," then explain why you want him to keep it up.

Forums are another avenue you should be exploring. Forums are online communities where people can ask questions and get helpful answers from other forum members. If you are very active on forums in your niche, the community of forum users may visit your blog to gain more insights and learn more about the topic. Use your blog's URL in your forum signature so that it's always visible in your forum posts.

RSS Distribution

Increase your popularity by letting others easily find your content through your RSS feed. Remember your RSS feed URL from our FeedBurner setup? Submit that URL to various RSS aggregating services to help get your content read by a wider audience. Here are a couple of URLs to check out.

- *http://www.millionrss.com*
- *http://feed2read.net*
- *http://feedboy.com*
- *http://www.feeds4all.com*
- *http://feedshark.brainbliss.com*
- *http://rss-feeds-submission.com*

Social Media Sites

Include your blog's URL on the profile pages for your Facebook, Plaxo, LinkedIn, YouTube, and Twitter accounts. These are all free services to help you connect and find friends. The more you participate on sites like these, the more potential traffic to your blog. Remember to follow those "Community Guidelines" we talked about earlier — no shameless promotion please.

Blogroll

WordPress provides an easy way to manage links through the administration dashboard. The links you display on your blog are sometimes called a "blogroll." Your blogroll is the collection of links you have chosen to display on your site. Most often this is done through the widgets dropdown found in the sidebar of the administration dashboard. You can find the Links dropdown in the sidebar as well.

You can add links to other blogs and sites in your niche, categorize them and add descriptions if you're so inclined. Once you have added your links, choose where you want to display the blogroll via the Widgets dropdown and place it either in the sidebar or the footer area of your blog.

You can exchange links with others, too. Have them add your site to their blogroll and do the same for them. The more sites link back to you, the higher your search engine ranking.

PROMOTIONAL CONSIDERATIONS

I would like to end the promotional section with a few words about what it is we are trying to accomplish. We are trying to get other blogs, sites, news organizations, social media outlets, TV shows, and everything else you can think of, to mention your articles or blog. The more this happens the more popular your blog. Maybe you're thinking to yourself "this really doesn't fit my profile," "I don't really want mainstream attention." That's certainly okay, but you can sell more product and become more respected in the field of your blog's topic if others are talking about you. And that talk doesn't have to be all good. Controversy can be huge for a blog, too.

MORE TO LEARN

THIS BOOK IS BUT A GUIDE to get you started blogging as quickly as possible while having the flexibility of a true stand-alone website. There is plenty more to learn when it comes to blogging — some specific to WordPress and some general advice that can apply to all bloggers. Your task now is to go find it. There are plenty of online resources to help you write better, help you promote your content, help you find stuff to write about, help find your voice, and much more.

SOME FINAL POINTS OF ADVICE

TRY TO REMEMBER THESE BULLET POINTS as you move along in your blogging endeavor.

- Be yourself – talk about what you know and give your personal perspective on the subject.
- Be consistent – write new articles at a consistent pace. If you're a once-a-week poster, then post once a week, not once a day for a month, then nothing for another month.
- Help your fellow blogger – comment and promote posts from others. They may return the favor, but even if they don't, being nice to others is good karma.
- Don't be afraid that what you say will be wrong. You may not know everything, in fact I'm sure you don't know everything, but that doesn't mean you don't have an opinion. Opinions don't have to be right or wrong, they just have to be yours.

And the most important point of advice is to have fun!

APPENDIX A

USE THIS APPENDIX to review WordPress version 2.8 user interface and functionality changes. I've only included the changes that are pretty major — changes that need to be documented so that you can follow along in the examples. Some minor changes have been excluded simply because they are aesthetic in nature. That said, here are a few of the major ones.

SCREEN OPTIONS

Version 2.8 of WordPress has redsigned the Screen Options dropdown and now allows you to not only turn on and off certain widgets for your dashboard, but also allows you to choose the number of columns to display in the broswer window.

This feature can be changed to suit your preference.

MANAGE PLUGINS

The plugin management screen has also changed slightly in version 2.8.

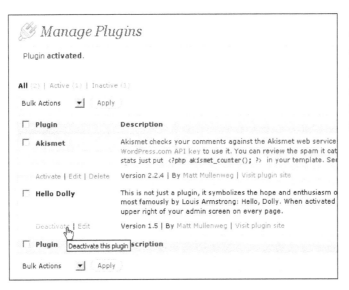

The new version shows the "Activate," "Edit," and "Delete" links all on the right side and shows your total number of active and inactive plugins at the top.

THEME INSTALLATION

In version 2.8 you can install themes in exactly the same manner as you did in version 2.7. However, Word-Press 2.8 has improved upon the installation by allowing you to find and install themes without ever leaving the WordPress administration dashboard. You don't need to find and download a zip file anymore.

> **NOTE:** *Not all themes are installable this way. You will still have to download zip files for premium themes, but if you're interested in finding a free theme, the built in search will do just fine.*

Find the Appearance dropdown in the administration dashboard sidebar and click on the "Add New Themes" link.

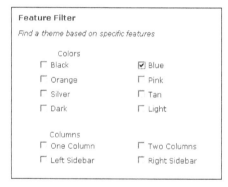

You'll notice that there is a feature filter in which you can select different options. Check the boxes for the features that you want your new theme to include.

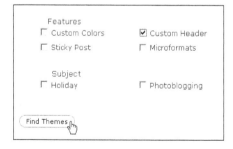

Click the "Find Themes" button to execute your search.

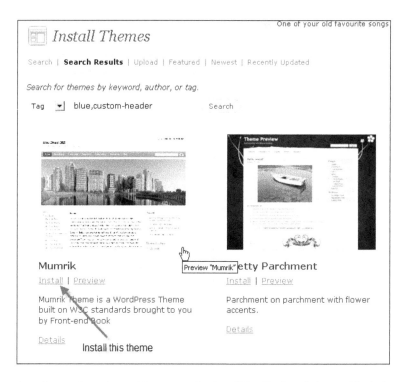

Any themes found matching your criteria will be displayed along with their thumbnail picture. Clicking on one of the thumbnails or the "Preview" link will allow you to see the theme larger and get a better picture of what the theme looks like.

If you like it, you can close the window and click on the "Install" link.

A small popup window will appear with an "Install Now" button at the bottom.

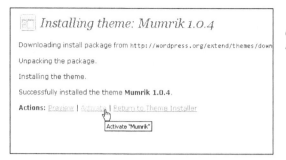

Once the theme is installed you will have to click the "Activate" link to have it go live on your site.

THEME WIDGETS

Theme widgets have also changed a bit. All of the widgets can be dragged to any sidebar location.

Version 2.8 also allows you to save widget settings for widgets that you are not currently showing on your blog. Version 2.7 would remove any text, or code you placed inside the widgets as you removed them from the sidebar locations.

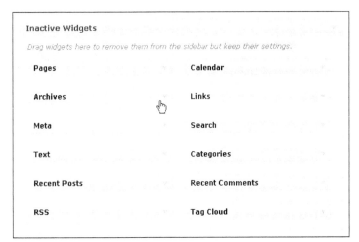

All of your widget locations are displayed on a single page so you can drag and drop them to any location from this one interface.

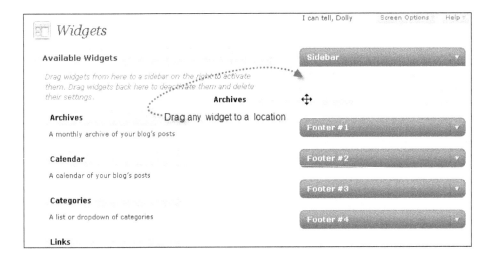

WORDPRESS UPGRADE PROCESS

The upgrade process for version 2.8.x is simplified and can be done in a couple of quick steps.

Make sure you use your WP Backup plugin to do a backup of your database. If there is a catastrophe (haven't seen one yet), you'll be glad you have a backup.

When you notice in your WordPress Dashboard that a new version is available, simply click on the "Please update now" link to begin the upgrade.

Go ahead and click on the "Upgrade Automatically" button to begin.

Your upgrade process should complete in a few seconds. Please be patient, it could take up to a minute or two depending on your hosting provider.

NOTES

www.ingramcontent.com/pod-product-compliance
Lightning Source LLC
Chambersburg PA
CBHW060155060326
40690CB00018B/4121